Animal
Tracks & Signs
of the Northwest

Alaska, Western Canada & the
Northwestern United States

Northern River Otter *Lontra canadensis* (BC)

J. Duane Sept

Calypso Publishing

Calypso Publishing   www.calypso-publishing.com
P. O. Box 1141
Sechelt, BC, Canada
VON 3A0
Duane Sept Photography   www.septphoto.com

Library and Archives Canada Cataloguing in Publication

Sept, J. Duane, 1950-
        Animal tracks and signs of the Northwest : Alaska, western
Canada & the northwestern United States / J. Duane Sept.

Includes bibliographical references and index.
ISBN 978-0-9739819-5-7

        1. Animal tracks--Northwest, Pacific--Identification.
2. Animal tracks--Canada, Western--Identification.
3. Animal tracks--Alaska--Identification. I. Title.

QL768.S47 2012   591.47'9   C2012-900199-6

Contents

Introduction

Something magical seems to happen when tracks appear where there was nothing merely hours earlier. Suddenly you realize that the maker of the tracks is likely still very close and perhaps watching you now! In fact, wildlife is all around us, passing nearby more often than we realize—but the substrate (earth, sand, snow, etc.) is not always the right consistency to record the occurrence.

This guide is an introduction to the exciting world of tracking. It can be a frustrating challenge to identify the owners of the tracks we encounter, and to determine what they were doing while they were making those tracks and why the tracks look so different in various substrates. But tracking is inspiring and rewarding, too, and it gives us a new awareness of the creatures who share our world.

Where space permits, both drawings and photographs of tracks have been included for the species in this guide.

Track Patterns

Most animals walk and run, but they also travel at many other rates in between. As mammals increase their speed, the way in which they move also changes, and these changes are represented in the surface along which they move. Track patterns and the distances between track groups dramatically increase as the animal moves faster. The measurements of these patterns often help to identify their maker.

The following illustrations summarize track patterns for several categories of gait typical of mammals.

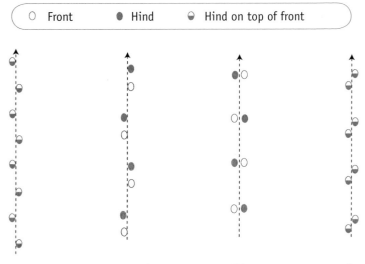

Direct Register Walking
Widespread

Overstep Walking
Typical of cats.

2x2 Walking
Northern Raccoon

2x2 Loping
Weasels, rats, and voles

4

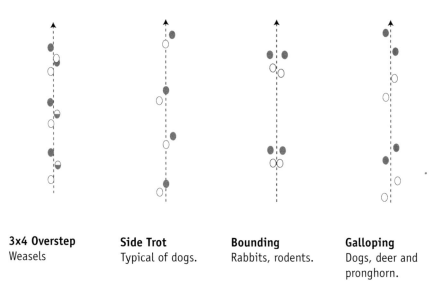

3x4 Overstep
Weasels

Side Trot
Typical of dogs.

Bounding
Rabbits, rodents.

Galloping
Dogs, deer and
pronghorn.

Additional gaits are also described in this guide for specific groups of mammals. For instance, bounding (jumping or hopping) is a term used for rodents and rabbits, and pronking is the distinctive bounding gait of the mule deer.

How to Use This Guide

Species Name Scientific Name
A common and a scientific name are listed for each species. Every living organism has a unique scientific name consisting of two parts: the genus (a grouping of species with common characteristics) and the species. Occasionally names change as new scientific information is discovered. The most current or appropriate name is included in this book. Common names are those used in everyday conversation by people who live in an area where the species occur, so some species have more than one common name. The most widely accepted common name appears at the top of each entry with the species' scientific name.

ANIMAL SIZE & WEIGHT
The size and weight of each species are included to assist in comparing animals with their respective track sizes.

TRACKS
Track sizes (both front and rear) for all species are included in the text. Some substrates, especially snow, may make tracks appear larger than they actually are. The track measurements included here include the nails and posterior pads for those animals that have them. Ungulate hooves are measured without the dewclaws, as these rarely register. Note that it is always best to take measurements of several tracks and

track groups, and to calculate an average size.

TRACK PATTERNS
Track patterns are an important element of species identification. In many cases they can also aid in determining the activities of the species. There are several gaits that mammals use in their day-to-day life. See page 4 to view many common gaits.

Stride
The stride is the distance between the tip of one footprint to the tip of the next print made by that foot.

Straddle
The straddle, or trail width, is an important measurement to take in the field. There is a direct relationship of the size of the animal to the width of the trail it creates.

Track Group Length
At least one track group length (or track pattern measurement, as it is sometimes called) is included for most species as well. This is the measurement of one full set of tracks made by all the feet, from the bottom edge of one set to the top edge of the same set.

Comments (Tracks)
Comments on tracks are included to give more detail to aid in identification of species.

SCAT
Scat measurements are an important part of species identification. Scats vary considerably from animal to animal depending on diet and moisture content of food. Scats from the same animal may also differ considerably in consistency. For instance, ungulates have different diets at different times of the year and as a result their droppings differ markedly. Information on size and shape of different scat types is included.

Comments (Scats)
Comments on scats are included to give more detail to aid in identification of species.

OTHER SIGN
Additional signs for most individual species are included in this guide.

HABITAT
The habitat, or type of landscape where an animal lives, is an important aid in identification. Many species only live in a very particular type of surroundings and conditions.

SIMILAR TRACKS & SIGN
Other species that may be mistaken for a particular animal are mentioned in this section.

Recording Your Observations

Fresh snow or the edge of a puddle can be all you need to gain insight into the world of our wild neighbors. But tracks are rarely perfect, so you may need to follow a trail for some time to get the best example(s). Take a photograph as well as the measurements of the tracks. Also make a note of the habitat where the tracks were found. All of these will help in identifying the maker.

It is important to make and record several measurements of the tracks you encounter. If possible, these should include track length and width for both the hind and front feet. The front and rear tracks are sometimes similar but sometimes very different. The track pattern measurement is simply the distance from the bottom edge of the rear track of one track group to the bottom edge of the next rear track group. The straddle or width of a trail is taken from the outer edges of both sides of an animal's tracks. Your data will be more precise if you measure many tracks and track patterns and calculate an average. Note that a ruler is printed on the back cover of this guide for convenient and accurate measuring of tracks and scats. Take along a small tape measure as well—it is another tool to help you get exact measurements of groups of tracks and track patterns.

Track Casting

Track casting is an easy way to bring home a life-size imprint of a track you have found in the wild. These casts make a great collection!

The technique is simple. Begin by placing a simple frame around your track, such as a piece of thin cardboard 1" (2.5 cm) wide that is long enough to completely surround your track while standing upright. Tape the two ends together so that it is able to hold the plaster. (Other materials can also work as a frame.) Mix plaster of Paris with enough water to make it the consistency of a milk shake. If the mixture is too watery, it will just take longer to dry. Pour your plaster over the track while it is inside your frame. Wait until it dries (usually 20 to 40 minutes) and then gently remove it. Be sure to record the information of where and when you found the original track.

Virginia Opossum *Didelphis virginiana*

Opossum Family (Didelphidae)
ANIMAL SIZE & WEIGHT
Total Length: 27–33" (69–84 cm)
Tail Length: 12–14" (30–36 cm)
Weight: 2.5–3.5 lb (1.1–1.6 kg)

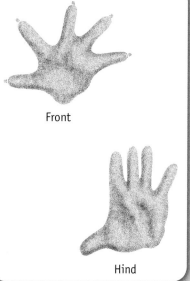

Front

Hind

The Virginia opossum is the only pouched mammal or marsupial found in North America, most common in the south. Its tail is prehensile, nearly naked and scaly. A young opossum can hang from its tail while in a tree. This species is nocturnal.

TRACKS
Front Print: Length: 1–2.3" (2.5–5.8 cm)
   Width: 1.25–2.5" (3.2–6.3 cm)
Hind Print: Length: 1.2–2.75" (3–7 cm)
   Width: 1.5–3 (3.8–7.6 cm)

TRACK PATTERN
Stride: Walking: 4.5–9" (11.4–22.9 cm)
Straddle: 3.75–5" (9.5–12.7 cm)
Track Group Length: Bounding: 9–11.5" (22.9–29.2 cm)
Comments: The front track, a very distinctive track, is often described as star-shaped, while the hind track looks similar to a human hand.

SCAT
Width: 0.4–1.1 (1–2.9 cm) in diameter
Length: 1–4.5 (2.5–11.4 cm)
Comments: Since opossums are omnivores, their diet changes often. As a result, their scat is quite variable.

OTHER SIGN
Den: Opossums take over dens abandoned by other animals. Occasionally they have even moved into a den that is still being occupied by the original owner.

HABITAT
Moist woodland and brushy areas near water.

Walking

American Pika *Ochotona princeps*

Pika Family (Ochotonidae)
ANIMAL SIZE & WEIGHT
Total Length: 7–7.75" (18–20 cm)
Tail Length: Absent
Weight: 6.1–8.1 oz (174–230 g)

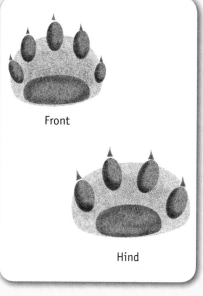

Front

Hind

The American pika is an active species that does not hibernate but instead remains busy under the snow during winter in deep snow conditions. Individuals gather, dry and store hay in piles during the summer and fall.

TRACKS
Front Print: Length: 0.7–0.9" (1.7–2.2 cm)
         Width: 0.7–0.9" (1.7–2.2 cm)
Hind Print: Length: 0.75–1.1" (1.9–2.9 cm)
         Width: 0.75–1" (1.9–2.5 cm)

TRACK PATTERNS
Stride: Walking: 4–10" (10–25 cm)
      Bounding: 2.25–15" (5.7–38.1 cm)

Bounding

Straddle: 2.5–3.5" (6.5–9 cm)
Track Group Length: Bounding: 2–4.9" (5.1–12.4 cm)
Comments: The track pattern left in the snow by an American pika resembles a small version of a rabbit or hare's tracks.

SCAT
Width: 0.09–0.13" (0.2–0.3 cm) in diameter
Comments: The droppings of the pika have been described as round pellets of black tapioca. These pellets are found among the rocks and boulders in their habitat. A second type of scat resembles freshly squeezed toothpaste ranging in color from dark green to black. This less common type may be present when the pika's food is quite soft.

OTHER SIGN
Hay Piles: In winter, little hay piles are left out to dry in the sun.
Scent Marking: Urine and pellets are often used for marking purposes. Urine stains can be seen in the snow near burrow entrances.

HABITAT
In talus slopes or large rocky areas in the mountains.

SIMILAR TRACKS & SIGN
Collard Pika *O. collaris*, a similar-looking species found in Alaska, is overall drab with grayish patches on the cheeks and a pale gray collar on the neck and shoulders.

9

Mountain Cottontail *Sylvilagus nuttallii*

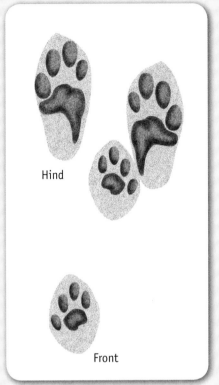

Hind

Front

Rabbit Family (Leporidae)
ANIMAL SIZE & WEIGHT
Total Length: 13–16" (33–41 cm)
Tail Length: 1.25–2.5" (3.2–6.4 cm)
Weight: 1.5–2.25 lb (680–1020 g)

The mountain cottontail is a small rabbit that does not hibernate during winter, but rather searches for the cambium of woody plants, conifer needles and occasionally berries. In spring and summer it feeds upon grasses and forbs. It does not change in color—unlike the snowshoe hare, which turns white in winter.

TRACKS
Front Print: Length: 1" (2.5 cm)
             Width: 0.8" (2 cm)
Hind Print: Length: 3.2" (8 cm)
             Width: 1" (2.5 cm)
TRACK PATTERNS
Stride: Walking: 7–12" (18–30 cm)
Straddle: 4–6" (10–15 cm)
Track Group Length: 6.5–11" (16.5–28 cm)
Comments: Both the front and rear tracks are highly asymmetrical. The rear tracks normally appear pointed at the tip of the track.
SCAT
Width: 0.1–0.25" (0.3–0.7 cm) in diameter
Length: 0.25–0.5" (0.6–1.3 cm)

Rabbit Family (Leporidae)

Comments: Rabbits and hares eat their pellets to help their intestinal bacteria digest the tough cellulose in their diets.

OTHER SIGN

Browse: Cottontails neatly clip the buds and twigs of shrubs within 2 feet (60 cm) from the ground.

HABITAT

Brushy areas and the edges where trees meet meadows.

SIMILAR TRACKS & SIGN

Eastern Cottontail *Sylvilagus floridanus* is a larger and darker species that was introduced from eastern North America and is now found in some areas in the West.

Snowshoe Hare *Lepus americanus* (see p. 12).

Scat is often deposited randomly. (ID)

Hopping (L) & Bounding (R)

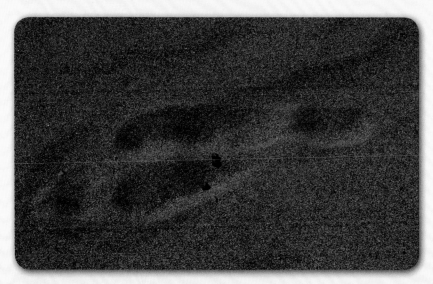

A set of mountain cottontail tracks and scat in sand. (ID)

11

Snowshoe Hare *Lepus americanus*

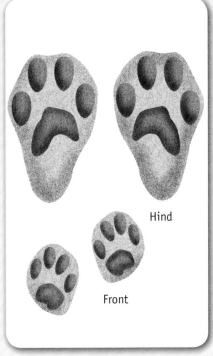

Hind

Front

Rabbit Family (Leporidae)
ANIMAL SIZE & WEIGHT
Total Length: 15–21" (38–53 cm)
Tail Length: 1.9–2.1" (4.8–5.4 cm)
Weight: 2.25–3.25 lb (1–1.5 kg)

The snowshoe hare is a familiar mammal to many people in North America. This animal is well adapted for a life in the snow with a changeable coat to match the seasons and built-in snowshoes on its feet. Females produce up to 4 young per year in the south, and as many as 12 young per year in the north. Predation on this species can cause up to 40 percent of a population to be taken by predators during the winter months. This is part of a natural 10-year cycle in which several interrelated predators and prey species undergo population fluctuations. One of the main predators of the snowshoe hare is the lynx (see p. 64). Others include the great horned owl, great gray owl, barred owl, goshawk, bobcat, red fox, coyote, wolf, black bear, mink and weasel.

TRACKS
Front Print: Length: 1.9–3" (4.8–7.6 cm)
⠀⠀⠀⠀⠀⠀**Width:** 1.1–2.25" (2.9–5.7 cm)
Hind Print: Length: 3.25–6" (8.3–15.2 cm)
⠀⠀⠀⠀⠀⠀**Width:** 1.6–5" (4.1–12.7 cm)

TRACK PATTERNS
Stride: Bounding: 8–72" (20.3–182.9 cm)
Straddle: 3.75–10" (9.5–25.4 cm)
Track Group Length: Bounding: 8–30" (20.3–76.2 cm)
Comments: The tracks of this hare are rounder than those of other rabbits. The nails may or may not register.

Rabbit Family (Leporidae)

SCAT

Width: 0.3–0.6" (0.8–1.4 cm) in diameter
Comments: In areas where other rabbits and hares are present, scat identification is not a reliable identification method, as the species' scat is indistinguishable.

OTHER SIGN

Browse: When hare browse, they leave precise 45-degree cuts that appear to be made with a knife. Deer browse, on the other hand, is rough and torn because deer do not have upper incisors. In summer, however, most rabbits and hares switch to a herb diet that includes clover, grasses and sedges.

HABITAT

Second-growth forests, swamps and shrubby areas.

SIMILAR TRACKS & SIGN

Mountain Cottontail (see p. 10).
Red Squirrel (see p. 20) are similar in snow but smaller.

Hopping (L) & Bounding (R)

Snowshoe hare browse. (AB)

Snowshoe hare scat. (AB)

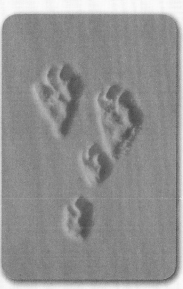

Perfect tracks in snow. (AB)

13

Yellow-pine Chipmunk *Tamias amoenus*

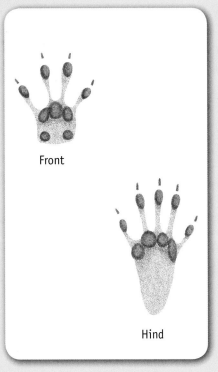

Front

Hind

Squirrel Family (Sciuridae)
ANIMAL SIZE & WEIGHT
Total Length: 7–9" (18–23 cm)
Tail Length: 3.25–4.25" (8.3–11 cm)
Weight: 1–2.5 oz (30–70 g)

The yellow-pine chipmunk is one of several species of chipmunks that can be encountered in the Northwest. It is small and brightly colored with reddish brown on its sides, 5 dark stripes on its back, and 3 dark and 2 light stripes on its face.

TRACKS
Front Print: Length: 0.8–1" (2–2.5 cm)
            Width: 0.4–0.8" (1–2 cm)
Hind Print: Length: 0.7–1.3" (1.8–3.3 cm)
            Width: 0.5–0.9" (1.3–2.3 cm)
TRACK PATTERNS
Stride: Running: 7–15" (18–38 cm)
        Straddle: 2–3.2" (5–8 cm)
Comments: The tracks of all chipmunks are too similar to be distinguished from each other.
SCAT
Width: 0.06–0.2" (0.2–0.5 cm) in diameter
Length: 0.2–0.4" (0.5–1 cm)
Comments: Chipmunk pellets are oblong and sometimes pointed at one end. A small collection can often be found where the animal was feeding.

OTHER SIGN
Burrows: Burrows 1.5–2" (3.8–5.1 cm) in diameter are often made in thick brush or rock piles. No soil is deposited at the entrance, so these burrows are quite difficult to find.

HABITAT
Coniferous mountain forests with rocky or bushy sites.

SIMILAR TRACKS & SIGN
Several chipmunks may be encountered in this area, but it is impossible to differentiate between individual species by their tracks and sign.

Least Chipmunk *Tamias minimus* is a smaller, drab-colored chipmunk.

Red-tailed Chipmunk *Tamias ruficaudus* is easily identified by the reddish underside of the tail.

Red squirrel / Douglas Squirrel (see p. 20) have larger tracks.

Bounding

A closeup of the front track of a yellow-pine chipmunk. (BC)

Golden-mantled Ground Squirrel
Spermophilus lateralis

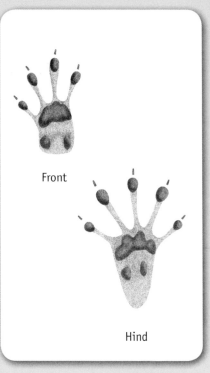

Front

Hind

Squirrel Family (Sciuridae)
ANIMAL SIZE & WEIGHT
Total Length: 11–13" (28–33 cm)
Tail Length: 3.75–4.75" (9.5–12 cm)
Weight: 6–12 oz (170–340 g)

The golden-mantled ground squirrel displays two black stripes and one white stripe on each side of its body and a white eye-ring. It looks like a large chipmunk but does not have any facial stripes. Chipmunks, on the other hand, always have a white stripe above and below their eye.

TRACKS
Front Print: Length: 0.9–1" (2.2–2.5 cm)
Width: 0.5–0.6" (1.3–1.4 cm)
Hind Print: Length: 0.9" (2.2 cm)
Width: 0.6–0.7" (1.4–1.7 cm)
Comments: The tracks of the many ground squirrel species are all very similar looking, and it is not possible to identify individual species.

TRACK PATTERN
Stride: Running: 7–20" (18–50 cm)
Straddle: 2.3–4" (5.8–10 cm)

SCAT
Width: 0.2–0.3" (0.5–0.8 cm) in diameter
Length: 0.2–0.5" (0.5–1.3 cm)

Comments: Scats are not deposited randomly as with other ground squirrels. This species places them on prominent perches and along their travel routes.

OTHER SIGN

Burrow: A short burrow is constructed, but the dirt excavated is removed from the entrance and deposited elsewhere.

HABITAT

Montane and sub-alpine forests.

SIMILAR TRACKS & SIGN

Columbian Ground Squirrel *Spermophilus columbianus* also is found in mountainous areas. It has a cinnamon buff back and no stripes.

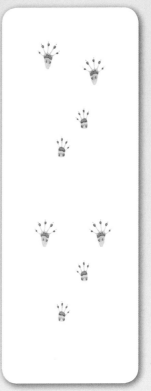

Running

Front track in soft sand. (BC)

Hoary Marmot *Marmota caligata*

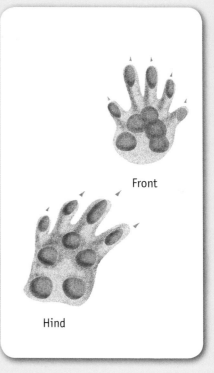

Front

Hind

Squirrel Family (Sciuridae)
ANIMAL SIZE & WEIGHT
Total Length: 27–32" (69–81 cm)
Tail Length: 7–9.25" (18–24 cm)
Weight: 11–15 lb (5–6.8 kg)

The hoary marmot is an alpine and sub-alpine resident. These marmots form loose colonies where they spend much of the year in hibernation. They must make the most of the warm days of the year in order to survive the long winter.

   This marmot lives in crevices among rocks or digs burrows with large obvious mounds located near vegetation. Their chief predators are golden eagles and grizzly bears. Their loud whistles can serve as a warning to others of impending danger, hence their alternate name, "whistler."

TRACKS
Front Print: Length: 2.1–3.1" (5.4–7.9 cm)
              Width: 1.25–2.6" (3.2–6.7 cm)
Hind Print: Length: 2–3.4" (5.1–8.6 cm)
             Width: 1.75–2.5" (4.4 –6.4 cm)
TRACK PATTERNS
Stride: Walking: 8–11" (20.3–27.9 cm)
         Bounding: 8–32" (20.3–81.3 cm)
Straddle: Walking: 5–7" (12.7–17.8 cm)
           Bounding: 4.75–7.5" (12.1–19.1 cm)
Track Group Length: Bounding: 4–16" (10.2–40.6 cm)
Comments: The heel of this species is hairless, so it may or may not register. The nails often do register.

SCAT
Width: 0.4–0.9" (1–2.4 cm) in diameter
Length: 1.5–3.5" (3.8–8.9 cm)
Comments: The hoary marmot uses an underground latrine, and as a result its scat is not usually observed.

OTHER SIGN
Dens: Dens may be dug from soil or in crevices among rocks.

HABITAT
This rodent requires a very specialized habitat—the rocky areas of alpine and sub-alpine regions. Occasionally, at the northern portion of their range, they are also found at lower elevations.

SIMILAR TRACKS & SIGN
Woodchuck _Marmota monax_ is a smaller, darker marmot of lower elevations that displays smaller tracks.

Walking (L) & Bounding (R)

Adult hoary marmot at burrow entrance. (AB)

Red Squirrel *Tamiasciurus hudsonicus*
Douglas Squirrel *Tamiasciurus douglasii*

Red squirrel

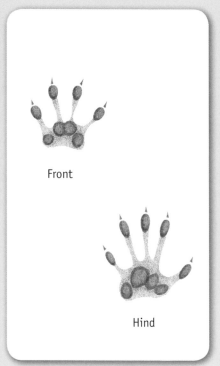

Front

Hind

Squirrel Family (Sciuridae)
ANIMAL SIZE & WEIGHT
Total Length: 11–14" (28–36 cm)
Tail Length: 4.25–5.75" (11–15 cm)
Weight: 6–11 oz (170–310 g)

The red and Douglas squirrels are very similar in most respects. The red squirrel is common, widespread and easy to recognize. Douglas squirrel is very similar except that its belly is light orange rather than white or gray. Its range is restricted to the Pacific Coast from California to British Columbia.

TRACKS
Front Print: Length: 1–1.25" (2.5–3.2 cm)
Width: 0.6–1" (1.4–2.5 cm)
Hind Print: Length: 0.9–2.25" (2.2–5.7 cm)
Width: 0.6–1.13" (1.6–2.9 cm)
TRACK PATTERNS
Stride: Walking: 3.5–5.25" (8.9–13.3 cm)
Bounding: 4–25" (10.2–63.5 cm)
Straddle: Walking: 2.4–2.75" (6–7 cm)
Bounding: 2.9–4.4" (7.3–11.1 cm)
Track Group Length: Bounding: 2–11" (5.1–27.9 cm)
Comments: The tracks of these squirrels in snow resemble rabbit tracks. Their size helps to distinguish the species.

Douglas squirrel in red.

20

Squirrel Family (Sciuridae)

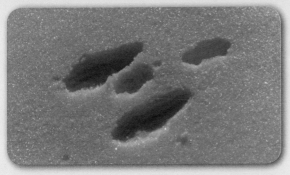

Tracks in snow are similar to those of the rabbit family but smaller. (AB)

SCAT
Width: 0.19–0.25" (0.5–0.6 cm) in diameter
Length: 0.19–0.4" (0.5–1.1 cm)
Comments: Red and Douglas squirrel scat varies in size and shape, and as a result it is not distinctive.

OTHER SIGN
Middens: Since these squirrels do not hibernate, they need to store an enormous amount of food for winter. A midden—the site where cone scales accumulate after the seeds have been removed—can exceed 2 feet (60 cm) in height. Underground dens may also be found associated with middens.

Bounding

HABITAT
Primarily boreal coniferous forests and mixed forests. These squirrels can also survive in towns and cities that have trees more than 40 years old.

SIMILAR TRACKS & SIGN
Eastern Gray Squirrel *Sciurus carolinensis* may also be encountered in urban areas. This gray or black squirrel was introduced from eastern North America and is now present in British Columbia to California. It often displays reddish tones in its fur and tail.

Western Gray Squirrel *Sciurus griseus* is a native species with a silvery-gray back, pure white belly and a long, bushy pepper-gray tail edged with white. Its range is from Washington to California.

A red squirrel midden and underground den. (BC)

Northern Flying Squirrel
Glaucomys sabrinus

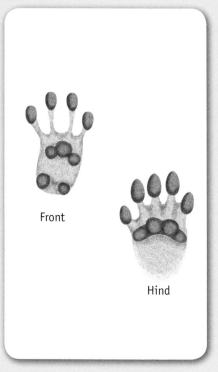

Front

Hind

Squirrel Family (Sciuridae)
ANIMAL SIZE & WEIGHT
Total Length: 9.75–15" (25–38 cm)
Tail Length: 4.25–7" (11–18 cm)
Weight: 2.6–6.5 oz (74–180 g)

The northern flying squirrel is a nocturnal species that glides from one location to another rather than actually flying. It has large eyes to aid in its nocturnal activities and large folds of skin that stretch between its hind legs and front legs to allow it to glide.

TRACKS
Front Print: Length: 0.7–1.25" (1.7–3.2 cm)
Width: 0.5–0.75" (1.3–1.9 cm)
Hind Print: Length: 1.25–1.9" (3.2–4.8 cm)
Width: 0.6–0.9" (1.6–2.4 cm)
TRACK PATTERNS
Stride: Bounding: 6–34" (15.2–86.4 cm)
Straddle: 2.75–4.25" (7–10.8 cm)
Track Group Length: 2–7" (5.1–17.8 cm)
Comments: On occasion, flying squirrels glide to the ground and leave a sitzmark (a landing spot in the snow). This is not often observed because flying squirrels normally climb down trees, rather than gliding from them.

SCAT
Width: 0.1–0.2" (0.2–.5 cm) in diameter
Length: 0.1–0.4" (0.3–1 cm)
Comments: Scat is normally deposited in hollow trees, where it accumulates over time.

OTHER SIGN
Nests: A hollow tree that contains an old woodpecker nest lined with soft materials is an excellent spot for northern flying squirrels to make a nest. Up to 15 individuals may be found in one nest, as these are very social animals.

HABITAT
Coniferous and deciduous forests with trees large enough for an old woodpecker's nest.

SIMILAR TRACKS & SIGN
Red Squirrel / Douglas Squirrel (see p. 20) has larger tracks, but in snow this difference can be difficult to determine.

Bounding

A truffle was removed from this location by a northern flying squirrel. (CA)

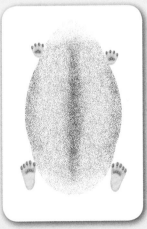

Sitzmark

Northern Pocket Gopher
Thomomys talpoides

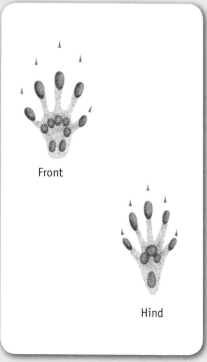

Front

Hind

**Pocket Gopher Family
(Geomyidae)**
ANIMAL SIZE & WEIGHT
Total Length: 7.5–10" (19–25 cm)
Tail Length: 1.6–3" (4.1–7.6 cm)
Weight: 2.6–7.4 oz (74–209 g)

The northern pocket gopher is the northern representative of several similar species found throughout North America. They are seldom observed, but the results of their digging activities are often seen.

TRACKS
Front Print: Length: 0.9–1.3" (2.3–3.3 cm)
Width: 0.4–0.5" (1.1–1.3 cm)
Hind Print: Length: 0.6–0.9" (1.5–2.2 cm)
Width: 0.4–0.7" (1.1–1.7 cm)
TRACK PATTERNS
Stride: Walking: 1.4–3" (3.5–7.6 cm)
Trotting: 3.5–4.1" (8.9–10.5 cm)
Straddle: Walking: 1.1–2" (2.9–5.1 cm)
Trotting: 1.4–1.5" (3.5–3.8 cm)
SCAT
Width: 0.1–0.2" (0.3–0.5 cm) in diameter
Length: 0.3–0.4" (8–11 cm)
Comments: The distinctive capsule-shaped scats have a smooth surface and are rounded at both ends.

SIGN

Eskers: A common sign left by the pocket gopher in the spring is the tubular "eskers" or trail castings (see photo). This snake-like sign indicates where the animal burrowed under the surface, an activity that is especially common during the winter months.

Dirt mounds: The pocket gopher creates dirt mounds that are much larger than those created by moles. Moles push dirt upwards (making a circular mound) while pocket gophers push dirt away from their burrow system (making a fan-shaped mound). Pocket gophers are also known for plugging their exits.

HABITAT

Various open habitats including grassy prairies, mountain meadows, fields, brushy areas and riverbanks with moist but not wet soils.

SIMILAR TRACKS & SIGN

Townsend's Mole *Scapanus townsendii* is a large mole that grows to 9.3" (24 cm) long and to 6 oz (170 g) in weight.

Coast Mole *Scapanus orarius* is a smaller species that grows to 7" (18 cm) long and to 3.2 oz (90 g) in weight.

Walking

This northern pocket gopher esker was found in spring. (AB)

25

American Beaver *Castor canadensis*

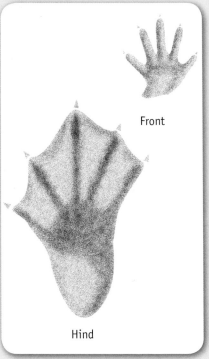

Front

Hind

Beaver Family (Castoridae)
ANIMAL SIZE & WEIGHT
Total Length: 3–4' (0.9–1.2 m)
Tail Length: 11–21" (28–53 cm)
Weight: 18–99 lb (8.2–45 kg)

The beaver is likely the most iconic mammal of North America. No other species is as captivating and intriguing. Although beavers are common and widespread, one must be patient and willing to take some time to observe these wonderful mammals. The amazing tail is one of its unique features. It is flat and scaly and often reaches 15" long and 7" wide (38 x 17.5 cm). It is quite versatile, with a host of uses: it serves as a rudder or sculling oar when swimming, a temperature regulator, a place to store fat over the winter, a stabilizing support when cutting down trees, and a tool for scaring away intruders or warning others of impending danger.

TRACKS
Front Print: Length: 2.5–3.9" (6.4–9.8 cm)
　　　　　　 Width: 2.25–3.5" (5.7–8.9 cm)
Hind Print: Length: 4.75–7" (12.1–17.8 cm)
　　　　　　 Width: 3.25–5.25" (8.3–13.3 cm)
TRACK PATTERNS
Stride: Walking: 6–11.5" (15.2–29.2 cm)
　　　　 Bounding: 10–32" (25.4–81.3 cm)
Straddle: Walking: 5.75–11" (14.6–27.9 cm)
　　　　　 Bounding: 6.75–13.5" (17.1–34.3 cm)
Track Group Length: Bounding: 7–14.5" (17.8–36.8 cm)
Comments: The large, flat tail of the beaver often

obliterates the tracks left by the front and rear feet.

SCAT
Width: 0.75–1.5" (1.9–3.8 cm) in diameter
Length: 1.25–3" (3.2–7.6 cm)
Comments: A beaver's scat is always filled with wood and plant fibres. It may be several pellets combined together or a single tubular scat.

OTHER SIGN
Many people are familiar with the distinctive large structures built by the industrious beaver—the lodge and dam. To create them, beaver cut small to fairly large trees leaving their signature stumps.

Scent Mounds: They also construct scent mounds by bringing up mud and debris from below the water's surface, placing it in a strategic position and depositing castoreum onto the mound. Castoreum is a strong scent, produced by the beaver's two musk glands, that is used for territorial communication.

HABITAT
Freshwater wetlands where there is suitable woody vegetation.

SIMILAR TRACKS & SIGN
Common Muskrat (see p. 28) tracks are smaller.

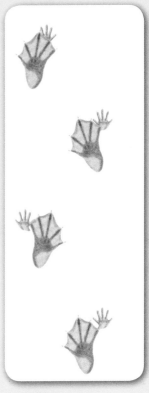

Walking

Beaver drag logs from the water onto land, leaving a trail. (AB)

Hind track. (AB)

Common Muskrat *Ondatra zibethicus*

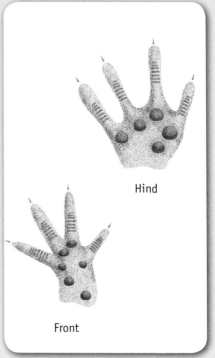

Hind

Front

Rats & Mice Family (Muridae)
ANIMAL SIZE & WEIGHT
Total Length: 18–24" (46–61 cm)
Tail Length: 8–11" (20–28 cm)
Weight: 1.7–3.6 lb (0.8–1.6 kg)

The muskrat is a common rodent that lives in a variety of wetlands but often goes unnoticed. It is considerably smaller than its wetland co-resident, the beaver. It builds a lodge by first heaping plant material into a large pile and then digging a burrow inside, creating a chamber within. Unlike beaver lodges, muskrat houses are built entirely of herbaceous vegetation and no branches.

Foods are primarily aquatic plants, especially cattails and bulrushes. The muskrat may also feed on fish, crustaceans, snails and occasionally young birds. The animal can remain submerged for up to 15 minutes when feeding. Its chief enemies include mink, raccoons, river otters and coyotes.

TRACKS
Front Print: Length: 0.9–1.5" (2.2–3.8 cm)
Width: 1–1.5" (2.5–3.8 cm)
Hind Print: Length: 1.5–2.75" (3.8–7 cm)
Width: 1.5–2.5" (3.8–6.4 cm)
TRACK PATTERNS
Stride: Walking: 3–7" (7.6–17.8 cm)
Loping: 1.6–4.5" (4.1–11.4 cm)
Hopping: 6–17" (15.2–43.2 cm)
Straddle: 3–5" (7.6–12.7 cm)

Track Group Length: Loping: 7.25–9.75" (18.4–24.8 cm)
Hopping: 3.5–6.5" (8.9–16.5 cm)

Comments: The nails are long and prominent in the tracks.

SCAT

Width: 0.2–0.25" (0.3–0.6 cm) in diameter
Length: 0.4–1" (1–2.5 cm)

Comments: Clusters of scat may be found in on logs in the water, on rocks or beaver dams, or on resting places along the shore.

OTHER SIGN

Homes: Muskrats commonly build lodges that are built entirely of herbaceous vegetation. They also build burrows in stream banks and similar locations.

Feeding Areas: The push-up is a type of feeding station made after freeze-up. Mud and aquatic plant material are placed over a hole in the ice allowing the muskrat to feed in safety inside this "miniature lodge."

HABITAT

A variety of wetlands including marshes and swamps and along streams, rivers and lakes.

SIMILAR TRACKS & SIGN

American Beaver (see p. 26) leaves much larger tracks.

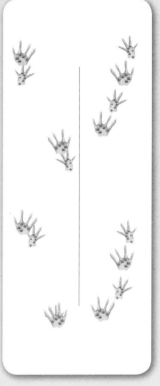

Walking (L) & Loping (R)

Muskrat scat and latrene. (AB)

Muskrat food includes a variety of vegetation. (NB)

Deer Mouse *Peromyscus maniculatus*

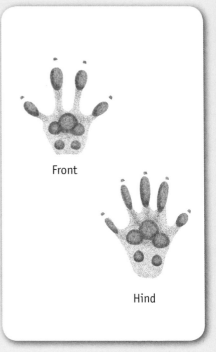

Front

Hind

Rats & Mice Family (Muridae)
ANIMAL SIZE & WEIGHT
Total Length: 5.5–8.25" (14–21 cm)
Tail Length: 2.1–4" (5.4–10 cm)
Weight: 0.6–1.25 oz (18–35 g)

The deer mouse is one of the most common small mammals found in North America. It has a home range of 0.3–4 acres (0.1–1.6 ha) or larger. Research has shown that a deer mouse displaced by 1 mile (1.6 km) will return to its home burrow within a single day.

TRACKS
Front Print: Length: 0.25–0.4" (0.6–1.1 cm)
Width: 0.3–0.5" (0.8–1.3 cm)
Hind Print: Length: 0.25–0.6" (0.6–1.4 cm)
Width: 0.3–0.5" (0.8–1.3 cm)
TRACK PATTERNS
Stride: Walking: 1.4–2.1" (3.5–5.4 cm)
Bounding: 4–20" (10.2–50.8 cm)
Straddle: Walking: 1–1.75" (2.5–4.4 cm)
Bounding: 1.25–1.75" (3.2–4.4 cm)
Track Group Length: Bounding: 1.1–2.1" (2.9–5.4 cm)
Comments: Mice are more easily identified by their track patterns than by their individual tracks. The tail track may or may not be obvious in snow.

SCAT
Width: 0.03–0.06" (0.1–0.2 cm) in diameter
Length: 0.09–0.2" (0.2–0.6 cm)

Rats & Mice Family (Muridae)

Comments: Deer mice leave their scat randomly, not at a latrine.

OTHER SIGN

Nests: These animals make a covered nest that is lined with soft plant material, fur, or wood and bark shavings. On average, each female produces three or four litters per year.

HABITAT

A wide variety of sites including grasslands, brushy areas and woodlands.

SIMILAR TRACKS & SIGN

House Mouse (see p. 37).

Walking (L) & Bounding (R)

Deer mice occasionally venture out on top of the snow in winter. A tail track is visible when the snow is deep. (AB)

Tracks in sand. (WA)

Meadow Vole *Microtus pennsylvanicus*

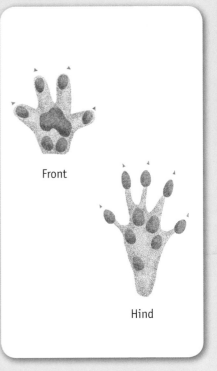

Front

Hind

Rats & Mice Family (Muridae)
ANIMAL SIZE & WEIGHT
Total Length: 5–7.5" (13–19 cm)
Tail Length: 1.25–1.75" (3.2–4.5 cm)
Weight: 0.6–2.25 oz (18–64 g)

The meadow vole is credited with being the most prolific mammal on earth. In addition it has one of the largest distributions of any small mammal in the world. It does not hibernate but stays active all year, especially just before sunset and in the early morning hours.

TRACKS
Front Print: Length: 0.25–0.4" (0.6–1.1 cm)
             Width: 0.3–0.6" (0.7–1.4 cm)
Hind Print: Length: 0.4–0.6" (1–1.6 cm)
             Width: 0.4–0.5" (1–1.4 cm)

TRACK PATTERNS
Stride: Walking: 1.25–1.9" (3.2–4.9 cm)
       Bounding: 4–9.25" (10.2–23.5 cm)
       2x2 Loping: 3–7" (7.6–17.7 cm)
       Trotting: 2–3.25" (5.1–8.3 cm)
       Hopping: 5.5–7" (14–17.8 cm)
Straddle: Walking: 1.25–2" (3.2–5.1 cm)
        Bounding: 1.2–1.5" (3–3.8 cm)
        2x2 Loping: 1–1.4" (2.5–3.5 cm)
        Hopping: 1.4–1.5" (3.5–3.8 cm)
Track Group Length: Hopping: 1.5–2" (3.8–5.1 cm)

Rats & Mice Family (Muridae)

Comments: In soft snow, the meadow vole drags its feet—but not its short tail. If there is heavy snow, it is unlikely to walk on the surface, preferring to remain inside its snowy tunnels. If snow is not too deep it will leave paired prints as it leaps, similar to the tracks of a weasel.

SCAT

Width: 0.06–0.13" (0.2–0.3 cm) in diameter
Length: 0.13–0.3" (0.4–0.8 cm)
Comments: Scat may be found along runs in the meadow vole's tunnels, and in the latrines away from its nest. Spring often reveals the tunnels that were covered with snow during the winter months.

OTHER SIGN

Winter Tunnels: Evidence of a winter nest may be discovered in the spring once the snow has melted. The nest is lined with grass and placed under the snow but above ground. Summer nests, however, are made below ground level.
Girdled Trees: Where food is scarce, voles may girdle trees below snow level.

HABITAT

In areas with long grass, including open grasslands near water and wet meadows.

SIMILAR TRACKS & SIGN

Creeping Vole *Microtus oregoni* is a similar-looking vole with a coastal range that extends from British Columbia to Oregon. Other species of voles are also found in the Northwest. All species leave similar signs.

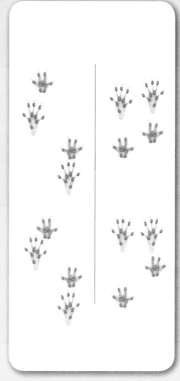

Walking (L) & Trotting (R)

Saplings girdled by meadow voles. (AB)

Meadow vole tracks in snow. (AB)

Bushy-tailed Woodrat *Neotoma cinerea*

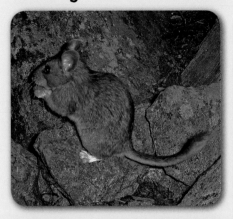

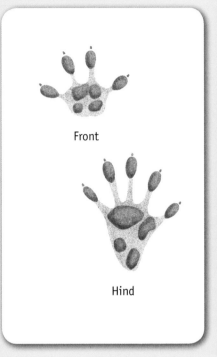

Front

Hind

Rats & Mice Family (Muridae)
ANIMAL SIZE & WEIGHT
Total Length: 11–18" (28–46 cm)
Tail Length: 4.4–8.75" (11–22 cm)
Weight: 2.75–18 oz (78–510 g)

Woodrats are easily identified by a light-colored belly. The bushy-tailed woodrat is the northern representative of the woodrat clan of North America. As its name suggests, it is graced with a large, bushy tail.

Also known as the packrat, this species has a well-known habit of collecting objects of interest for its "collection." These items may even come from your campsite. In its place, the woodrat leaves an item it has selected to replace the item it removes. In the morning, when you reach out to grab your jewellery, you may find a bone or pinecone neatly left in its place.

TRACKS
Front Print: Length: 0.5–1" (1.3–2.5 cm)
Width: 0.6–0.9" (1.4–2.4 cm)
Hind Print: Length: 0.5–1.25" (1.6–3.2 cm)
Width: 0.6–1" (1.4–2.5 cm)
TRACK PATTERNS
Stride: Walking: 2–3.5" (5.1–8.9 cm)
Bounding: 4–8" (10.2–20.3 cm)
Straddle: Bounding: 2.1–2.75" (5.4–7 cm)
Track Group Length: 3.5–6.5" (9–16.5 cm)
Comments: The nails of this rodent normally do not register.
SCAT
Width: 0.13–0.19" (0.3–0.5 cm) in diameter

Length: 0.3–0.6" (0.8–1.6 cm)

Comments: At rocky sites there may be an accumulation of dung that is tar-like in consistency and as large as 6" (15 cm) or more in diameter. The dung may drip over a cliff edge, along with urine stains that are likely territorial markings.

OTHER SIGN

Nests: In central British Columbia I found a bushy-tailed woodrat nest reaching an impressive 6' (1.8 m) in height (see photo). The nest is normally made in a rock cleft, abandoned building or similar site. If such a spot is not available, a tree-supported lodge may be constructed. The nest I found was likely used by several generations of bushy-tailed woodrats.

HABITAT

In fields, pastures, woods, groves and mixed woods.

SIMILAR TRACKS & SIGN

Norway Rat (see p. 36).

Walking (L) & Bounding (R)

A bushy-tailed woodrat soaked this stick with urine to mark its territory. (BC)

A large bushy-tailed woodrat nest. (BC)

Norway Rat *Rattus norvegicus*

Rats & Mice Family (Muridae)
ANIMAL SIZE & WEIGHT
Total Length: 13–18" (33–46 cm)
Tail Length: 4.75–8.75" (12–22 cm)
Weight: 7–17 oz (200–480 g)

Accidentally introduced from Europe, the Norway rat is now distributed globally. This species has been destructive to human dwellings and food, as well as being the vectors of the plague and other diseases. The Norway rat has a dark belly and a hairless tail.

TRACKS
Front Print: Length: 0.5–0.9" (1.3–2.2 cm)
Width: 0.5–0.75" (1.3–1.9 cm)
Hind Print: Length: 0.75–1.4" (1.9–3.5 cm)
Width: 0.6–1.2" (1.6–3 cm)

TRACK PATTERNS
Stride: Walking: 3–5" (7.6–12.7 cm)
Straddle: Walking: 1.6–2.75" (4.1–7 cm)
Track Group Length: Bounding: 2.4–4" (6–10.2 cm)
Comments: This species is most often found in or near dwellings and agricultural activity in the human environment, so that is where its tracks are likely to be seen.

SCAT
Width: 0.13–0.19" (0.3–0.5 cm) in diameter
Length: 0.25–0.6" (0.7–1.4 cm)
Comments: The scat of the Norway rat is not very symmetrical. Bushy-tailed woodrat (see p. 34) scat is much more symmetrical.

OTHER SIGN
Nests: The Norway rat often chews through human-made structures to gain access to shelter and make a nest constructed of any soft materials available.

HABITAT
An introduced species found in human environments, including houses, sheds and similar locations.

SIMILAR TRACKS & SIGN
Roof Rat *Rattus rattus* is a similar species with larger ears and a longer, hairless tail. Its tracks and signs are not distinguishable from those of the Norway rat.
Bushy-tailed Woodrat (p. 34) tracks are similar, but woodrats rarely associate with buildings in use by humans.

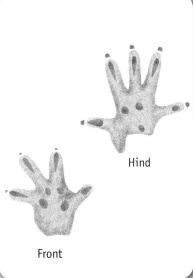

Hind

Front

Walking

House Mouse *Mus musculus*

Rats & Mice Family (Muridae)
ANIMAL SIZE & WEIGHT
Total Length: 5–7.75" (13–20 cm)
Tail Length: 2.5–4" (6.3–10 cm)
Weight: 0.5–0.9 oz (14–25 g)

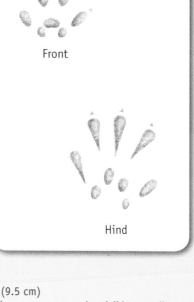

Front

Hind

As its common name suggests, the house mouse is a familiar species that invades residences and other structures in the human environment. Originally from Europe, this species is now common throughout most of North America. This mouse has a gray, long and hairless tail.

TRACKS
Front Print: Length: 0.6" (1.5 cm)
Width: 0.8" (2 cm)
Hind Print: Length: 1.1" (2.8 cm)
Width: 0.9" (2.3 cm)
Straddle: 0.75" (1.9 cm)
Track Group Length: 3.75" (9.5 cm)
Comments: The tracks of a house mouse may be visible on spilt flour or perhaps dust in the basement.

SCAT
Length: 0.1–0.25" (0.3–0.6 cm)
Comments: Scats are elongated with pointed ends.

OTHER SIGN
Nests: Nests may be found in any areas that are accessible to this mouse. Soft materials are used to line the nest.

HABITAT
This introduced species is found in houses, sheds and similar locations in the human environment.

SIMILAR TRACKS & SIGN
Norway Rat (see p. 36) is a larger mammal found in a similar habitat.

Running

North American Porcupine
Erethizon dorsatum

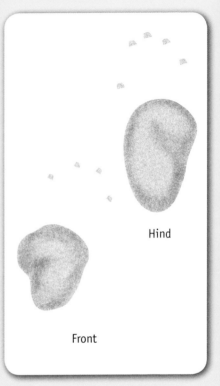

Hind

Front

Porcupine Family (Erethizontidae)
ANIMAL SIZE & WEIGHT
Total Length: 21–41" (53–104 cm)
Tail Length: 5.5–9" (14–23 cm)
Weight: Usually 10–28 lb (4.5–12.6 kg); one record over 50 lb (22.5 kg)

The porcupine is a slow-moving creature that is often observed in the shortened daylight hours of winter, feeding high up in a tree. During the summer, however, it is usually nocturnal. Porcupines feed primarily on the bark of conifers, birch and willow in winter, and on various herbs during the summer months.

In a ravine, I once heard loud cries that sounded to me like a dog in distress. Upon investigation I found a pair of porcupines that were courting—I had been hearing the mating call. Others who have heard this call have described it as similar to the moaning sound made by a cub bear, or the "screams" and cries of a baby. It is a truly unforgettable vocalization.

TRACKS
Front Print: Length: 2.25–3.4" (5.7–8.6 cm)
　　　　　　 Width: 1.25–1.9" (3.2–4.8 cm)
Hind Print: Length: 2.75–4" (7–10.2 cm)
　　　　　　 Width: 1.25–2" (3.2–5.1 cm)
TRACK PATTERNS
Stride: Walking: 6–10.5" (15.2–26.7 cm)
　　　　Straddle: 5–9" (12.7–22.9 cm)

Porcupine Family (Erethizontidae)

Comments: The tracks of the porcupine reveal the characteristic pebbly surface of its feet in mud or other soft surfaces. In the deep snow of winter, it leaves a very distinctive trail somewhat like a deep plowed furrow.

SCAT
Width: 0.25–0.5" (6–1.3 cm) in diameter
Length: 0.5–1.25" (1.3–3.2 cm)
Comments: At the den site, scat can be very abundant.

OTHER SIGN
Dens: Porcupines normally den in areas with some type of overhang and a good food supply close by.
Browse: Twigs are cut at a 45-degree angle with coarse incisor marks. Birch and willow are among their preferred foods. Porcupine scat is often found at the base of the tree they feed on.

HABITAT
A wide range of areas including coniferous, deciduous and mixed-wood forests as well as grasslands.

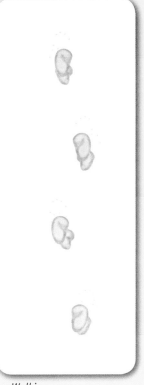

Walking

Porcupine tracks in deep snow. (AB)

Porcupine scat. (AB)

Coyote *Canis latrans*

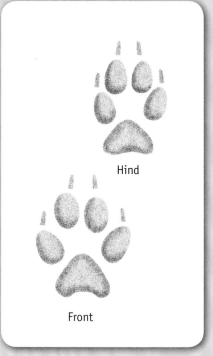

Hind

Front

Dog Family (Canidae)
ANIMAL SIZE & WEIGHT
Total Length: 3.5–4.5' (1.1–1.4 m)
Tail Length: 12–16" (30–41 cm)
Weight: 18–44 lb (8.2–20 kg)

The song of the coyote is always a special treat to hear in the wild. The coyote is a smart and cunning predator that is often taken for granted. In cities these smart predators have learned that humans provide food and have lost their fear of man. Caution should always be exercised with young children in areas with coyotes.

The first time I watched a coyote feeding on berries, I was quite surprised. I thought coyotes only fed on mammals, but in fact they consume a wide variety of foods including squirrels, mice, hares, birds, bird eggs, amphibians, reptiles, berries and vegetation. They are smart opportunists—a key point in how they thrive in spite of man's persistence to get rid of them!

TRACKS
Front Print: Length: 2.25–3.25" (5.7–8.3 cm)
Width: 1.5–2.5" (3.8–6.4 cm)
Hind Print: Length: 2.1–3" (5.4–7.6 cm)
Width: 1.1–2 (2.9–5.1 cm)
TRACK PATTERNS
Stride: Walking: 11–17" (27.9–43.2 cm)
Loping: 5–20" (12.7–50.8 cm)
Trotting: 15–21" (38.1–53.3 cm)
Galloping: 12–90" (30.5–228.6 cm)
Straddle: Walking: 4–5.5" (10.2–14 cm)
Trotting: 2.25–4" (5.7–10.2 cm)

Dog Family (Canidae)

Track Group Length: Loping: 26–33" (66–83.8 cm)
Galloping: 35–101" (88.9–2.6 m)
Comments: Western coyote tracks are larger than those of individuals in eastern North America.
SCAT
Width: 0.4–1.4" (1–3.5 cm) in diameter
Length: 5–13" (12.7–33 cm)
Comments: There is some overlap in the size of coyote scats with other members of the dog family: the wolf and the red fox.
OTHER SIGN
Beds: Beds approximately 21" (53 cm) in diameter may be found.
Dens: Dens are often placed on a slope covered with brush. Former dens of the American badger or woodchuck have also been widened to 1 ft (30 cm) in diameter to accommodate the new owners. More than one opening to the den is not uncommon.
Predation: Evidence of predation sometimes provides more information on the activities of the coyote.
HABITAT
All terrains south of the tundra and often even in our cities.
SIMILAR TRACKS & SIGN
Gray Wolf (p. 42) is larger, with much larger feet.
Domestic Dog (see p. 70).

Overstep (L) & Side trot (R)

A perfect pair of coyote tracks in a side trot. (AB)

Coyote scat. (AB)

Gray Wolf *Canis lupus*

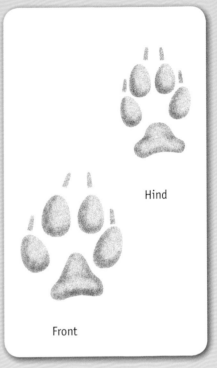

Hind

Front

Dog Family (Canidae)
ANIMAL SIZE & WEIGHT
Total Length: 4.5– 6.5' (1.4–2 m)
Tail Length: 14–20" (36–51 cm)
Weight: 57–170 lb (26–77 kg)

This large member of the dog family is often referred to as the timber wolf. Its diet consists primarily of large mammals including white-tailed deer, mule deer, moose, caribou, mountain sheep and beavers. The distinctive call of one or more wolves in the evening is always memorable. More often than not, fleeting glimpses are the only sight that we have of a wolf.

This predator hunts alone, but more often in a pack of up to 30 animals. Only the alpha (dominant) female will breed in years when there is sufficient food to sustain the pack. In years where there is insufficient food, no breeding takes place.

TRACKS
Front Print: Length: 3.75–5.75" (9.5–14.6 cm)
　　　　　　Width: 2.9–5" (7.3–12.7 cm)
Hind Print: Length: 3.75–5.25" (9.5–13.3 cm)
　　　　　　Width: 2.6–4.5" (6.7–11.4 cm)
TRACK PATTERNS
Stride: Walking: 13–24" (33–61 cm)
　　　Loping: 20–23" (50.8–58.4 cm)
　　　Trotting (direct register): 22–34" (55.9–86.4 cm)
　　　Galloping: 6–68" (15.2–1.7 m)

Dog Family (Canidae)

Straddle: Walking:6–10" (15.2–25.4 cm)
  Trotting (direct register): 4–9.25" (10.2–23.5 cm)
Track Group Length: Loping: 40–49" (1.02–1.25 m)
  Galloping: 55–99" (1.4–2.52 m)
Comments: The largest gray wolf track ever measured was found on the Porcupine River, Alaska, by Olaus Murie. The track had a width and length of 6.5" (16.5 cm). Alaskan mammals overall are larger and so are their tracks.

SCAT

Width: 0.5–1.9" (1.3–4.8 cm) in diameter
Length: 6–17" (15.2–43.2 cm)
Comments: A wolf track is easily confused with that of the domestic dog. One method to determine tracks are not those of a dog is by evaluating the likelihood of a person and/or a pet dog being present at the site.

OTHER SIGN

Dens: Wolf dens are usually dug by pregnant females, in light or sandy ground, often by the side of a sandy or gravelly embankment or ridge, at an elevated location near water. Such a den is only used for a short time, just until the pups are large enough to accompany the pack.
Scent posts: Various objects (small bushes, tree trunks, rocks, blocks of ice, etc.) are used as markers on which wolves place their scent. Sometimes a single animal leaves the marks, other times all members of pack leave them.

Overstep (L) & Trotting (R)

HABITAT

The gray wolf is found in the arctic tundra and various forests.

SIMILAR TRACKS & SIGN

Coyote (see p. 40) tracks are normally smaller.
Domestic Dog (see p. 70).

Front track of a gray wolf. (AB)

43

Red Fox *Vulpes vulpes*

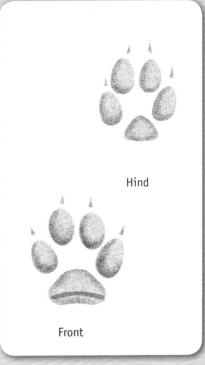

Hind

Front

Dog Family (Canidae)
ANIMAL SIZE & WEIGHT
Total Length: 35–44" (89–112 cm)
Tail Length: 14–17" (36–43 cm)
Weight: 8–15 lb (3.6–6.8 kg)

The red fox is a familiar, easily recognized mammal. One of several color variations may be encountered, including the "cross fox" with darker hairs along the back and the shoulder blades, and the "silver fox," which is mainly black with silver-tipped hairs. All color phases display a bushy tail with a white tip. This omnivore dines on small rodents, rabbits, birds, invertebrates, birds, eggs, fruits and berries.

TRACKS
Front Print: Length: 1.9–2.9" (4.8–7.3 cm)
　　　　　　Width: 1.4–2.1" (3.5–5.4 cm)
Hind Print: Length: 1.6–2.5" (4.1–6.4 cm)
　　　　　　Width: 1.25–1.9" (3.2–-4.8 cm)

TRACK PATTERNS
Stride: Walking: 8–12" (20.3–30.5 cm)
　　　　Loping: 9–15" (22.9–38.1 cm)
　　　　Trotting: 13–20" (33–50.8 cm)
　　　　Galloping: 8–109" (20.3–2.8 m)
Straddle: Trotting: 2–3.75" (5.1–9.5 cm)
Track Group Length: Loping: 20–29" (50.8–73.7 cm)
　　　　　　　　　　Galloping: 25–60" (63.5–1.5 m)

Comments: The red fox track is distinctive, if it is a clear track with good details. The heel pad includes a chevron-shaped bar in the palm pad of the front track.

Dog Family (Canidae)

The walking pattern of the red fox is easily recognized by its distinctiveness—almost a straight line. Each mark represents two tracks: the forefoot, overprinted with the hind foot. Since the nails are semi-retractable, they may or may not register.

SCAT
Width: 0.3–0.75" (0.8–1.9 cm) in diameter
Length: 3–6" (7.6–15.2 cm)
Comments: A good print will reveal an inverted V-shaped, callused ridge across the pad, in the heel pad. This identifying feature is not found in other canines.

OTHER SIGN
Dens: Red fox dens are 7–9" (17.5–22.5 cm) in diameter. In the spring the den is in use, and a pile of loose dirt is normally seen in front, unless the foxes are using a rock crevice or cave.
Scent Posts: The red fox leaves urine with a skunk-like scent on prominent objects on or beside the trail, in order to mark its territory. This odor can be detected up to 30 ft (9 m) away under ideal conditions.

HABITAT
In open fields and pastures with brushy areas.

SIMILAR TRACKS & SIGN
Gray Fox *Urocyon cinereoargenteus* is a southern species with tracks that lack the bar impression in the palm pad of the front track.
Domestic Dog (see p. 70).

Walking (L) & Trotting (R)

Front track of a red fox. (SC)

The distinctive track pattern of the red fox. (SC)

American Black Bear *Ursus americanus*

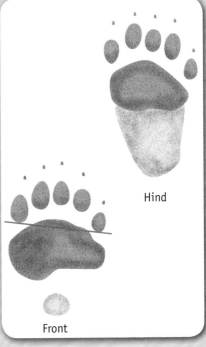

Hind

Front

Bear Family (Ursidae)
ANIMAL SIZE & WEIGHT
Total Length: 4.5–6' (1.4–1.8 m)
Tail Length: 3.25–7" (8.3–18 cm)
Weight: 88–595 lb (40–270 kg)

The familiar black bear is not always black as its common name indicates. It can also be cinnamon, from western North America; bluish, from Alaska; and white, from northern and coastal British Columbia.

This common omnivore is found throughout most of North America. During winter, the American black bear's heartbeat drops from about 40 beats per minute to 10, and its oxygen intake is reduced by 50 percent. Its metabolism also slows down, but its body temperature drops only a few degrees. Females may lose up to 30 percent of their fall body weight while nursing their young over the winter months.

TRACKS
Front Print: Length: 3.75–8" (9.5–20.3 cm)
　　　　　　Width: 3.25–6" (8.3–15.2 cm)
Hind Print: Length: 5.4–8.9" (13.7–22.5 cm)
　　　　　　Width: 3.5–6" (8.9–15.2 cm)
TRACK PATTERNS
Stride: Walking (direct register): 17–25" (43.2–63.5 cm)
　　　　Walking (overstep): 19–28" (48.3–71.1 cm)
　　　　3x Loping: 25–30" (63.5–76.2 cm)
　　　　Galloping: 24–60" (61–1.5 cm)
Straddle: 8–14" (20.3–35.6 cm)
Track Group Length: 3x Loping: 38–50" (96.5–1.3 m)
　　　　　　　　　　Galloping: 49–75" (1.2–1.9 m)

Bear Family (Ursidae)

Comments: An effective method to determine whether a bear track is from a black or a grizzly is to look at the length of the nails on the front feet. The nails of a black bear are shorter than the length of its toe. The nails of the grizzly, however, are equal or greater. In addition, the toes of the black bear are arranged to form more of an arc.

SCAT

Width: 1.25–2.5" (3.2–6.4 cm) in diameter
Length: 5–12" (12.7–30.5 cm)
Comments: Scat is extremely variable depending upon the diet of the individual. The diet may include fish, vegetation, berries or other fruit.

OTHER SIGN

Digs: Both black bears and grizzlies excavate for ants, insect larvae and small mammals.
Dens: In preparation for winter, black bears may excavate a den under the roots of a tree, or den inside a pile of brush, in a large hollow log or under fallen trees.
Bear Trees: Bears use trees in two ways. They often strip the bark from conifers including spruce, pine and fir trees to eat the cambium and sap underneath. They also use rubbing trees, rubbing against them possibly to relieve itching. These trees may also be sign or scent posts of some type.
Predation: Both black bears and grizzlies cover their kills with any material available to protect them from scavengers.

HABITAT

Primarily in forested areas, where it thrives, and also in mountains, swamps, marshes and thickets.

SIMILAR TRACKS & SIGN

Grizzly Bear (see p. 48).

Overstep (L) & Loping (R)

American black bear scat. (BC)

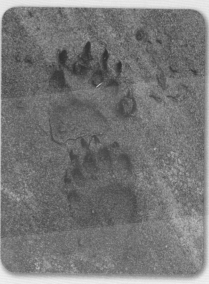

American black bear tracks. (BC)

47

Grizzly Bear *Ursus arctos*

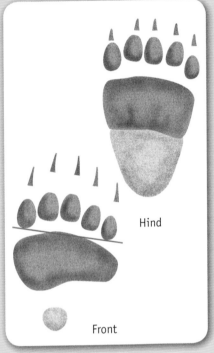

Hind

Front

Bear Family (Ursidae)
ANIMAL SIZE & WEIGHT
Total Length: 6–8.5' (1.8–2.6 m)
Tail Length: 3–7" (7.6–18 cm)
Weight: 242–1160 lb (110–530 kg); occasionally to 1656 lb (750 kg)

The grizzly bear is easily identified by the presence of a pronounced hump on its shoulders. It is a large species whose vertical reach extends to 12 ft (3.6 m). As a result, if you climb a tree because you feel threatened by a grizzly, you will need to climb higher than that to stay out of reach of an adult grizzly. Young grizzlies, however, can climb trees!

TRACKS
Front Print: Length: 7–13.5" (17.8–34.3 cm); rarely to 16" (40.6 cm)
Width: 5–8.75" (12.7–22.2 cm)
Hind Print: Length: 8.25–14" (21–35.6 cm)
Width: 4.6–8.5" (11.7–21.6 cm)

TRACK PATTERNS
Stride: Walking (direct register): 19–29" (48.3–73.7 cm)
Walking (overstep): 25–42" (63.5–106.7 cm)
3x Loping: 18–33" (45.7–83.8 cm)
Galloping: 30–35" (76.2–88.9 cm)
Straddle: Walking (direct register): 13–20" (33–50.8 cm)
Walking (overstep): 10–19" (25.4–48.3 cm)
Track Group Length: 3x Loping: 59–87" (1.5–2.21 m)
Galloping: 85–95" (2.16–2.41 m)
Comments: In some areas, trails have been established in which individual bears place their tracks

exactly where other bears have gone over many years. These mark trails have been documented for American black bears and grizzlies (see photo).

SCAT

Width: 1.25– 2.9" (3.2–7.3 cm) in diameter
Length: 7–20" (17.8–50.8 cm)
Comments: As with the black bear, scat can vary greatly from elongated to patty-shaped depending upon the nature of the food.

OTHER SIGN

Dens: Grizzlies normally dig their own dens, beginning from early September to mid-November, and they enter their dens between mid-October and mid-November. They emerge between late March and early May.

Digs: Grizzlies dig for tasty tubers, insect larvae, and small mammals using their long foreclaws. Large pits often indicate the presence of a grizzly digging for a burrowing mammal such as a ground squirrel or marmot.

Bear Trees: Like American black bears, grizzlies use trees as scratching or rubbing posts, possibly to relieve itching or to mark territory, or both. Grizzlies also strip the lower bark of spruce, pine and fir trees to get at the sap.

Predation: Grizzlies cover their kills with branches, fresh earth or other forest debris to conceal a carcass. If you come across such a situation, the bear is near and is likely to defend its food cache.

HABITAT

The majestic grizzly bear is present in the tundra, high mountains, alpine and sub-alpine forests, and along coastlines.

SIMILAR TRACKS & SIGN

American Black Bear (see p. 46).

Direct Register (L) & Loping (R)

Grizzly bear tracks in soft sand. (BC)

A grizzly bear mark trail. (BC)

Northern Raccoon *Procyon lotor*

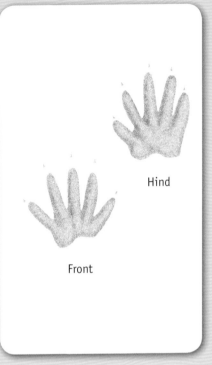

Hind

Front

Raccoon Family (Procyonidae)
ANIMAL SIZE & WEIGHT
Total Length: 26–38" (66–97 cm)
Tail Length: 7.5–11" (19–28 cm)
Weight: 12–31 lb (5.4–14 kg)

The raccoon is a familiar mammal in North America, well known for its playfulness. This omnivore seeks out fruit, nuts, corn and other garden crops as well as carrion. It is an extremely adaptable mammal that has adjusted to many habitats and proximity to humans.

TRACKS
Front Print: Length: 1.75–3.1" (4.4–7.9 cm)
　　　　　　 Width: 1.5–3.25" (3.8–8.3 cm)
Hind Print: Length: 2.1–3.9" (5.4–9.9 cm)
　　　　　　 Width: 1.5–2.6" (3.8–6.7 cm)

TRACK PATTERNS
Stride: Walking (2x2): 8–19" (20.3–48.3 cm)
　　　　 Walking (direct register): 8–14" (20.3–35.6 cm)
　　　　 Bounding: 10–30" (25.4–76.2 cm)
Straddle: Walking (2x2): 3.5–7" (8.9–17.8 cm)
　　　　　 Walking (direct register): 3.5–6" (8.9–15.2 cm)
Track Group Length: Bounding: 15–27" (38.1–68.6 cm)
Comments: There are few tracks that can be confused with those of the raccoon in this area.

SCAT
Width: 0.3–1.2" (0.8–3 cm) in diameter

Raccoon Family (Procyonidae)

Length: 3.5–7" (8.9–17.8 cm)

Comments: Raccoon scats vary greatly in shape from tubular to patty-shaped, depending upon the animal's diet. They are easily confused with those of skunks or bear cubs. Do not handle the scats as they can contain a parasitic roundworm, *Baylisascaris procyonis*, which can be fatal to people.

OTHER SIGN

Den: A den may be located in a rock crevice or cave, under an abandoned building or in a disused fox den.

HABITAT

Near forested areas close to waterways and river valleys, as well as brush areas; also in cities, suburbs and rural areas.

SIMILAR TRACKS & SIGN

The tracks of the northern raccoon are unique.

Walking (L) & Fast Walk (R)

This raccoon has been dining on cherries. (BC)

A pair of northern raccoon tracks. (SC)

Northern River Otter *Lontra canadensis*

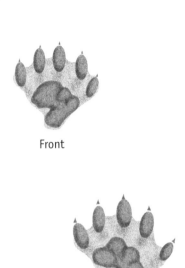

Front

Hind

Weasel Family (Mustelidae)
ANIMAL SIZE & WEIGHT
Total Length: 3.5– 4.5" (1.1–1.4 m)
Tail Length: 12–20" (30–51 cm)
Weight: 10–24 lb (4.5–11 kg)

The northern river otter is a water-loving carnivore that feeds primarily on fish, crayfish, turtles and frogs. It is well known for its playfulness and has been observed sliding on snow banks for more than 25' (7.5 m). It will also take advantage of wet mud for sliding. The northern river otter is normally found near water but may also travel far distances away from water.

TRACKS
Front Print: Length: 2.1–3.25" (5.4–8.3 cm)
　　　　　　Width: 1.9–3" (4.8–7.6 cm)
Hind Print: Length: 2.1–4" (5.4–10.2 cm)
　　　　　　Width: 2.1–3.75" (5.4–9.5 cm)
TRACK PATTERNS
Stride: Walking: 5.75–14" (14.6–35.6 cm)
　　　　3x4 Loping: 6–28" (15.2–71.1 cm)
　　　　2x2 Loping: 15–40" (38–101.6 cm)
Straddle: 4.5–7" (11.4 –17.8 cm)
Track Group Length: 3x4 loping: 10–20.5" (25.4–52.1 cm)
Comments: The nails often do not register in tracks.
SCAT
Width: 0.38–1" (1–2.5 cm) in diameter
Length: 3–6" (7.6–15.2 cm)
Comments: Irregular and sometimes scattered in shape, and often includes fish bones. Its color closely

matches the food—reddish for crabs, and black to silver for fish.

OTHER SIGN

Slides: A slide or rolling area is often a sign that otters have been present.

Den: A permanent den is frequently made in a bank. Here the animals use both underwater and land entrances for security. Resting areas and additional den sites, such as abandoned muskrat, beaver or woodchuck dens, are also used, but these are not permanent.

HABITAT

Wooded areas near rivers, ponds, lakes and the ocean.

SIMILAR TRACKS & SIGN

American Mink (see p. 58) also plays in snow and mud, but its tracks are much smaller.

Walking (L) & Loping (R)

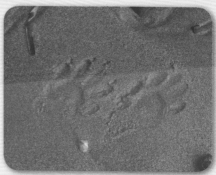

Tracks on a sandy beach. (WA)

A northern river otter slide in snow. (BC)

American Marten *Martes americana*

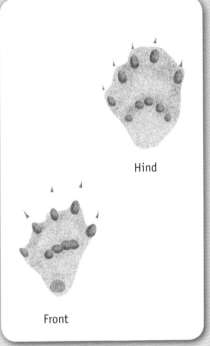

Hind

Front

Weasel Family (Mustelidae)
ANIMAL SIZE & WEIGHT
Total Length: 19–26" (48–66 cm)
Tail Length: 5.5–7.25" (14–18 cm)
Weight: 1.25–2.75 lb (0.6–1.2 kg)

The sleek coat of the American marten does not change to white in winter as our weasels' do. It is yellow to dark brown overall, often with a throat patch of white to orange fur.

This species is an opportunistic feeder that hunts both day and night. Its varied diet includes squirrels, hares, bird eggs and chicks, insects, carrion and occasionally berries. It is also known for its sweet tooth.

TRACKS
Front Print: Length: 1.6–2.75" (4.1–7 cm)
Width: 1.3–2.6" (3.3–6.7 cm)
Hind Print: Length: 1.5–2.75" (3.8–7 cm)
Width: 1.2–2.25" (3–5.7 cm)
TRACK PATTERNS
Stride: Walking: 5–9" (12.7–22.9 cm)
3x4 Loping: 8–32" (20.3–81.3 cm)
2x2 Loping: 10"–6' (25.4 cm–1.83 m)
Straddle: 3x4 Loping: 3.25–5.5" (8.3–13.3 cm)
2x2 Loping: 2.5–4.5" (6.4–11.4 cm)
Track Group Length: 3x4 Loping: 8.5–20" (21.6–50.8 cm)
2x2 Loping: 3.5–7.5" (8.9–19.1 cm)
Comments: Females are smaller in size, thus the tracks

Weasel Family (Mustelidae)

with measurements at the low end of the range will likely be those of a female. All members of the weasel family form a twin-print pattern when traveling in deep snow.

SCAT

Width: 0.2–0.6" (0.5–1.6 cm) in diameter
Length: 2–5" (5.1–12.7 cm)
Comments: Marten scat is long and thin, sometimes twisted, and composed primarily of small rodent hair, small bones and berry seeds when in season. Weasels are not known to eat berries.

OTHER SIGN

Food Caches: Marten are known to store surplus food in caches for short periods of time.
Dens: Hollow trees, rock crevices and similar sheltered spots are normal locations for a marten den. Soft vegetation normally lines their home.

HABITAT

In mature coniferous forests.

SIMILAR TRACKS & SIGN

Long-tailed Weasel (see p. 56) have a similar track pattern, but they live primarily in grasslands and deciduous forests rather than coniferous forests.
Fisher *Martes pennanti* is a larger member of the weasel family, that reaches 40" (102 cm) long. Its larger front tracks measure 2.1-3.8" (5.4-9.8 cm) long and 1.8-4.25" (4.8-10.8 cm) wide.

Walking (L) & Loping (R)

American marten scat. (AB)

Long-tailed Weasel *Mustela frenata*

Weasel Family (Mustelidae)
ANIMAL SIZE & WEIGHT
Total Length: 13–19" (33–48 cm)
Tail Length: 4.75–7.5" (12–19 cm)
Weight: 3–14 oz (85–400 g)

Hind

The long-tailed weasel's tail is tipped with black year-round. This species dines on voles and mice, ground squirrels, wood rats, red squirrels, rabbits and shrews, as well as the eggs and young of ground-nesting birds. This weasel has declined in numbers and is therefore not as easy to find as it once was.

Front

TRACKS
Front Print: Length: 0.6–1.4" (1.6–3.7 cm)
Width: 0.75–1.2" (1.9–3 cm)
Hind Print: Length: 0.75–1.5" (1.9–3.8 cm)
Width: 0.6–1" (1.4–2.5 cm)
TRACK PATTERNS
Stride: Bounding: 15–25" (38.1–63.5 cm)
2x2 Loping: 10–45" (25.4 – 114.3 cm)
Straddle: Bounding: 1.9–2.9" (4.8–7.3 cm)
Track Group Length: Bounding: 6–11" (15.2–27.9 cm)
Comments: The nails may or may not register on the substrate.
SCAT
Width: 0.2–0.4" (0.5–1 cm) in diameter
Length: 1–3.25" (2.5–8.3 cm)
Comments: All weasels form latrines near their nests.
OTHER SIGN
Burrows: Burrow openings in snow approximately 3" (7.6 cm) wide are another sign that this species is present.
HABITAT
Sea level to alpine areas including open grasslands, river bottoms, woodlands and alpine tundra.
SIMILAR TRACKS & SIGN
Short-tailed Weasel (see p. 57).

Walking

Short-tailed Weasel *Mustela erminea*

Weasel Family (Mustelidae)
ANIMAL SIZE & WEIGHT
Total Length: 8.25–13" (22–33 cm)
Tail Length: 1.6–3.5" (4.1–8.9 cm)
Weight: 1.6–3.75 oz (46–106 g)

In this species, as in all true weasels, the winter coat changes to white to match the color of the snow. The short-tailed weasel is often referred to as the ermine. Its short tail is tipped with black year-round. Young females are sexually mature at two to three months. Males, however, are not sexually mature until they are 10 or 11 months old.

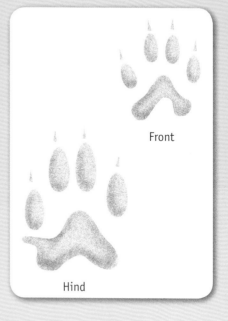

Front

Hind

TRACKS
Front Print: Length: 0.4–0.6" (1.0–1.6 cm)
             Width: 0.4–0.6" (1.0–1.6 cm)
Hind Print: Length: 0.4–0.6" (1.0–1.4 cm)
             Width: 0.4–0.75" (1–1.9 cm)
TRACK PATTERNS
Stride: 2x2 Galloping: 4–40" (10.2–101.6 cm)
Straddle: 2x2 Galloping: 0.9–1.9" (2.2–4.8 cm)
Track Group Length: 1.5–2.3" (3.8–5.8 cm)
Comments: Female weasels are noticably larger than males and so are their tracks. Individuals from Alaska are larger, and their measurements are not included here. The tracks of short-tailed weasels are not a definitive way to identify this species.
SCAT
Width: 0.1–0.3" (0.3–0.8 cm) in diameter
Length: 0.75–2.4" (1.9–6 cm)
Comments: Just as the tracks of least weasels and long-tailed weasels overlap, so too do their scats.
OTHER SIGNS
Dens: Burrows and nests of mice, ground squirrels, chipmunks and pocket gophers are often modified and converted into dens by short-tailed weasels.
HABITAT
Open fields, pastures, woods, groves, mixed woods.
SIMILAR TRACKS & SIGN
Long-tailed Weasel (see p. 56)
Least Weasel *Mustela nivalis* is a smaller species that lacks a black tip on its tail.

2x2 Loping

American Mink *Mustela vison*

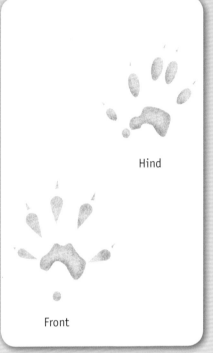

Hind

Front

Weasel Family (Mustelidae)
ANIMAL SIZE & WEIGHT
Total Length: 17–24" (43–61 cm)
Tail Length: 5–8.25" (13–21 cm)
Weight: 1.75–5 lb (0.8–2.3 kg)

The pelage of the American mink is brown to black overall except for white spots on the chest, chin and occasionally the belly. This widespread carnivore eats a variety of small mammals, fish, reptiles, amphibians and birds. It makes its den in a site near water, including under tree roots, piles of brush or logs, or in muskrat or beaver dens in banks.

TRACKS
Front Print: Length: 1.1–1.9" (2.9–4.8 cm)
　　　　　　　Width: 0.9–1.75" (2.2–4.4 cm)
Hind Print: Length: 0.8–1.75" (2.1–4.4 cm)
　　　　　　　Width: 0.9–1.6" (2.4–4.1 cm)
TRACK PATTERNS
Stride: Walking: 3.5–7.75" (8.9–19.7 cm)
　　　　Bounding: 11–26" (27.9–66 cm)
　　　　2x2 Loping: 9–50" (22.9 cm–1.2 m)
Straddle: 2x2 Loping: 2–3.75" (5.1–9.5 cm)
　　　　　Sliding: 3–5" (7.6–12.7 cm)
Track Group Length: 3x4 Loping: 5–14" (12.7–35.6 cm)
　　　　　　　　　　Bounding: 5–16" (12.7–40.6 cm)
Comments: Their nails may or may not register with their tracks.

58

SCAT

Width: 0.25–0.4" (0.6–1 cm) in diameter
Length: 1–4" (2.5–10.2 cm)
Comments: Scat of mink is twisted, tapered at both ends and often folded as well. This species is similar to other members of the weasel family, but its wetland habitat will help in identifying it. Also like other members of the weasel family, the American mink tends to place its scat on prominent objects such as rocks and stumps along the routes it uses.

OTHER SIGN

Dens: Mink are known to take over a muskrat lodge or bank burrow after making a meal of the young and sometimes the adults that they found inside.
Slides: Mink, like their close relative the otter, appear to have a fun-loving nature and may slide along level snow down embankments or through the snow into water.

HABITAT

Near various wetlands including marshes, streams, rivers, lakes, ponds, forest edges and tidal flats.

SIMILAR TRACKS & SIGN

Northern River Otter (see p. 52) live in similar habitats, but their tracks are larger.

Walking (L) & 2x2 Loping (R)

Typical lope of an American mink. (CA)

American Badger *Taxidea taxus*

Weasel Family (Mustelidae)
ANIMAL SIZE & WEIGHT
Total Length: 31–33" (79–84 cm)
Tail Length: 5–6.25" (13–16 cm)
Weight: 11–24 lb (5–11 kg)

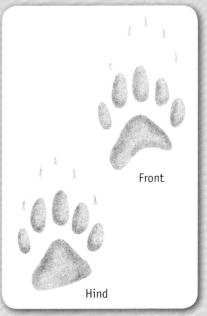

Front

Hind

The American badger is an impressive creature. A close look at its front feet and claws tells the story. The size of its front claws alone indicate that this mammal is a digging machine—so much so that badgers are often referred to as nature's rototillers and backhoes. The badger is a carnivore that catches its dinner by digging out its prey: various ground squirrels and prairie dogs.

TRACKS
Front Print: Length: 2.9–3.9" (7.3–9.8 cm)
　　　　　Width: 1.6–2.6" (4–6.7 cm)
Hind Print: Length: 1.9–2.75" (4.8–7 cm)
　　　　　Width: 1.4–2" (3.5–5.1 cm)
TRACK PATTERN
Stride: Walking: 5.5–9.75" (14–24.8 cm)
　　　Loping: 10–12" (25.4–30.5 cm)
　　　Trotting: 10–15" (25.4–38.1 cm)
Straddle: Walking: 5–7.5" (12.7–19.1 cm)
　　　　Trotting: 3–6" (7.6–15.2 cm)
Track Group Length: Loping: 17–20" (43.2–50.8 cm)
Comments: The size of the long claws on the front tracks are very distinctive. In addition, the track of the hind foot is quite small in comparison with that of the front.

SCAT
Width: 0.4–0.75" (1–1.9 cm)
Length: 3–6" (7.6–15.2 cm)
Comments: Scat is not often found above ground since it is normally deposited in burrows.
OTHER SIGN
Den: A badger often digs its own den, or it may take over a ground squirrel's burrow.
HABITAT
Primarily the open grasslands of the parkland and prairies.

Walking

Striped Skunk *Mephitis mephitis*

Skunk Family (Mephitidae)
ANIMAL SIZE & WEIGHT
Total Length: 21–31" (53–79 cm)
Tail Length: 8.6–12" (22–30 cm)
Weight: 4.25–9.25 lb (1.9–4.2 kg)

The striped skunk needs no introduction. It is an omnivore that feeds on insects, fruits and berries, small mammals, bird eggs and nestlings, amphibians, reptiles, grains and green vegetation. The scent glands normally have about 1 oz (30 ml) of noxious chemicals inside.

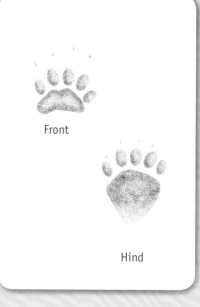

Front

Hind

TRACKS
Front Print: Length: 1.6–2" (4–5.2 cm)
          Width: 1–1.2" (2.5–3 cm)
Hind Print: Length: 1.3–2" (3.3–5.1 cm)
          Width: 0.9–1.2" (2.4–3 cm)
TRACK PATTERNS
Stride: Walking (direct register): 4–8"
    (10.2–20.3 cm)
    Walking (overstep): 5.75–9" (14.6–22.9 cm)
Straddle: 3–4.5" (7.6–11.4 cm)
Track Group Length: Loping: 8–16.5" (20.3–42 cm)
Comments: Skunks' feet are small and rather dainty, and as a result so are their tracks. The heel portion of the rear track rarely registers.
SCAT
Width: 0.4–0.9" (1–2.2 cm) in diameter
Length: 2–5" (5.1–12.7 cm)
Comments: The striped skunk often forms latrines at various sites.
OTHER SIGN
Digs: Striped skunks are one of many animals that create digs, so it can be tricky to identify the digger. Skunks usually dig for insects and their larvae.

Bird's Nest Predation: Striped skunks eat eggs from birds' nests, often but not always leaving crushed eggs and nests in shambles. They are not tidy eaters!

HABITAT
Most types of habitat except the driest areas.
SIMILAR TRACKS & SIGN
Western Spotted Skunk *Spilogale gracilis* is much smaller with spots.

Walking Overstep

Mountain Lion *Puma concolor*

Hind

Front

Cat Family (Felidae)
ANIMAL SIZE & WEIGHT
Total Length: 5–9' (1.5–2.7 m)
Tail Length: 20–35" (51–89 cm)
Weight: 70–190 lb (32–86 kg)

The mountain lion is known by several names including cougar and puma. It is our largest cat with a long and graceful tail. This impressive feline is not observed often even by those who spend a great deal of time in the woods. More often its call is heard—a sound that is not easily forgotten. It is a loud screaming and moaning sound that can carry long distances when conditions are right. This cat is capable of preying on a variety of mammals including white-tail and mule deer.

TRACKS
Front Print: Length: 2.75–3.9" (7–9.8 cm)
　　　　　　　Width: 2.9–4.9" (7.3–12.4 cm)
Hind Print: Length: 3–4.1" (7.6–10.5 cm)
　　　　　　　Width: 2.6–4.9" (6.5–12.4 cm)
TRACK PATTERNS
Stride: Walking (direct register): 15–28" (38.1–71 cm)
　　　　Walking (overstep): 19–32" (48.3–81.3 cm)
　　　　3x Loping: 45–55" (1.14–1.4 m)
　　　　Trotting: 29–38" (73.7–96.5 cm)
　　　　Galloping: 3–25' (91.4–762 cm)
Straddle: Walking (direct register): 4–11" (10.2–27.9 cm)
　　　　　Walking (overstep): 5–9" (12.7–22.9 cm)
　　　　　Trotting: 3–5.5" (7.6–14 cm)

Cat Family (Felidae)

Track Group Length: 3x Loping: 40–50" (1.02–1.27 m)
Trotting: 3–5.5" (7.6–14 cm)
Galloping: 50–75" (1.27–1.9 m)

Comments: The front tracks of the mountain lion are larger, rounder and less symmetrical than the rear tracks.

SCAT

Width: 0.75–1.6" (1.9–4.1 cm) in diameter
Length: 6.5–17" (16.5–43.2 cm)

Comments: The scat is variable depending upon what part of its prey the animal has eaten. Little hair or bone will be present on the scat when the mountain lion has eaten from the liver, heart or other organs of a large ungulate like a deer.

Mountain lions will cover their scat on occasion, but more often they do not. The uncovered scat may be left as a scent post.

OTHER SIGN

Dens: Female mountain lions select den sites to have their young, usually a site that provides protection from heavy rain and hot sun. This can be the edge of a rocky cliff or outcropping, or under fallen logs. This den may be used for several years.

Scrapes: Boundaries are marked with a series of scrapes—piles of dirt, or similar material—that are marked with urine and scat.

Walking (L) & Overstep (R)

HABITAT

Remote wooded areas that have rocky sections nearby.

SIMILAR TRACKS & SIGN

Canada Lynx (see p. 64).

Front track of a mountain lion in soft sand. (BC)

Canada Lynx *Felis lynx*

Front

Hind

Cat Family (Felidae)
ANIMAL SIZE & WEIGHT
Total Length: 31–40" (79–102 cm)
Tail Length: 3.5–4.75" (8.9–12 cm)
Weight: 15–40 lb (6.8–18 kg)

The Canada lynx is a true creature of the north. It relies heavily on populations of snowshoe hare and also feeds on squirrels, grouse and other rodents. This cat some-times caches its meat by covering it with snow or leafy debris.

TRACKS
Front Print: Length: 2.4–4.25" (6–10.8 cm)
Width: 2.4–5.6" (6–14.3 cm)
Hind Print: Length: 2.5–4.1" (6.4–10.5 cm)
Width: 2.1–5" (5.4–12.7 cm)

TRACK PATTERNS
Stride: Walking: 11–18" (27.9–45.7 cm)
Walking (overstep): 14–19.5" (35.6–49.6 cm)
Trotting: 19–25" (48.3–63.5 cm)
Galloping: 45–65" (114–1.65 m)
Straddle: Walking: 5–9.5" (12.7–24.1 cm)
Walking (overstep): 5–8" (12.7–20.3 cm)
Trotting: 5–6.5" (12.7–16.5 cm)
Track Group Length: Galloping: 36–60" (91.4–152.4 cm)
Comments: Note that the toes on the hind feet are longer than those on the front, so hind foot impres-sions are longer and larger than those of the front foot. There is also a tremendous amount of fur

Cat Family (Felidae)

between the toe and palm pads, which often makes it difficult to find a clear track imprint.

SCAT
Width: 0.5–0.9" (1.3–2.4 cm) in diameter
Length: 3–10" (7.6–25.4 cm)
Comments: Scats are often deposited on elevated surfaces—even if only a slight elevation. Juveniles are believed to be the main individuals that cover their scat.

OTHER SIGN
Scrapes: Territories are posted with a series of scrapes (piles of dirt) or similar material that is marked with urine.

Predation: The Canada lynx may or may not cover its kill. This feline is not known to have a preference.

HABITAT
Northern coniferous forests.

Direct Register (L) & Galloping (R)

Fresh track in powder snow. (BC)

The sit spot of a lynx before moving on. (BC)

Bobcat *Felis rufus*

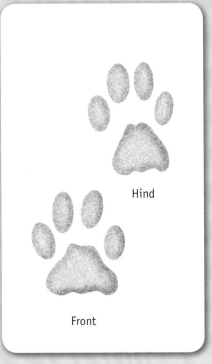

Hind

Front

Cat Family (Felidae)
ANIMAL SIZE & WEIGHT
Total Length: 30–49" (76–124 cm)
Tail Length: 5–6.75" (13–17 cm)
Weight: 9–40 lb (4.1–18 kg)

The bobcat, like all cats, is not commonly observed in the wild. Its tracks are often the only way its presence is revealed. This species is very similar to the lynx, but the lynx favors areas with high snowfall in winter.

Bobcats sometimes cover their kills. Other species that do so include lynx, cougar, fisher and bears. Bobcats do most of their hunting by night. Their prey includes rabbits, squirrels, rats, mice, voles, beavers, skunks and occasionally deer.

TRACKS
Front Print: Length: 1.6–2.5" (4.1–6.4 cm)
Width: 1.4–2.6" (3.5–6.7 cm)
Hind Print: Length: 1.6–2.5" (4–6.4 cm)
Width: 1.2–2.6" (3–6.7 cm)

TRACK PATTERNS
Stride: Walking (direct register): 11.25–23" (28.6–58 cm)
Walking (overstep): 12–18" (30.5–45.7 cm)
2x2 Loping: 24–71" (61–180 cm)
Trotting: 15–26" (38.1–66 cm)
Galloping: 16–48" (40.6–121.9 cm)
Straddle: Walking (overstep): 3.75–5" (9.5–12.7 cm)
2x2 Loping: 2.5–4" (6.4–10.2 cm)
Trotting: 3–4.5" (7.6–11.4 cm)

Cat Family (Felidae)

Track Group Length: Galloping: 35–65" (88.9–165.1 cm)

Comments: The nails are retractable as with all cats and often do not register, except when the animal is walking on slippery surfaces, climbing or chasing its prey. The front track has a larger metacarpal (triangular, flattened) area than the hind track.

SCAT

Width: 0.6–0.75" (1.6–1.9 cm) in diameter
Length: 2–5" (5–12.7 cm)
Comments: Bobcat scat often displays a definite segmented appearance. Large bone fragments are not present as in coyote or wolf scat. Cats often cover their scat, but not always.

OTHER SIGN

Predation: Bobcat will often cover a kill if it is not able to consume it all. It will use its forepaws to cover the carcass with forest debris or even snow. Some individuals, however, do not cover their prey.

HABITAT

Coniferous and deciduous forests, in areas that do not receive large volumes of snow in winter.

Direct Register (L) & Overstep (R)

SIMILAR TRACKS & SIGN

Domestic Cat (see p. 71) strides are noticeably smaller. The location of the tracks will often help in identifying tracks.

Bobcat tracks in dried sand.

Harbor Seal *Phoca vitulina*

Hair Seal Family (Phocidae)
ANIMAL SIZE & WEIGHT
Total Length: 4–6.6' (1.2–2 m)
Weight: to 289 lb (130 kg)

The harbor seal is a marine mammal that regularly visits its "haul-outs"—sites where they venture onto land. These sites provide a safe haven for anywhere from a few to hundreds of individuals while the tide is out, but most haul-outs are reclaimed by the sea when the tide returns. The harbor seal can remain submerged up to 23 minutes and dive to 980' (294 m) deep.

TRACKS
Front Print: Length: 8–12" (20.3–30.5 cm)
           Width: 7–10" (17.8–25.4 cm)
TRACK PATTERNS
Stride: N/A
Straddle: Approx. 3.5' (1.05 m)
Comments: The trails of the harbour seal are distinctive as a result of their body drag.

SCAT
Width: to 1.5" (3.8 cm) in diameter
Comments: Scat is not normally found as it is usually deposited in water.
OTHER SIGNS
No other sign may be found for this species.

HABITAT

In coastal waters including bays, harbors, estuaries and mudflats, and upstream a short distance in streams that drain into the ocean.

SIMILAR TRACKS & SIGN

California Sea Lion *Zalophus californianus* and **Steller's Sea Lion** *Eumetopias jubatus* are much larger marine mammals. Both rarely inhabit land frequented by people.

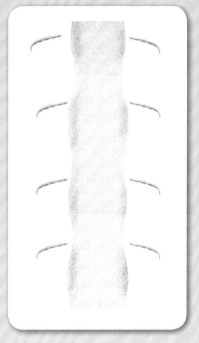

Walking

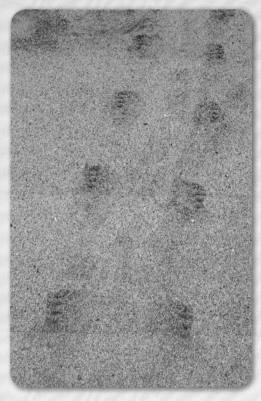

The track pattern of the harbor seal is distinctive. (CA)

Domestic Dog *Canis familiaris*

Dog Family (Canidae)
ANIMAL SIZE & WEIGHT
Total Length: 14.2–57.1" (36–1.4 m)
Tail Length: 5.1–20.1" (13–51 cm)
Weight: 2.2–174 lb (1–79 kg)

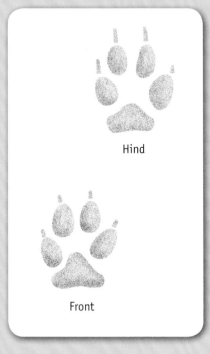

Hind

Front

The familiar pet dog that many people have in their homes frequently accompanies us on our trips outdoors, and as a result domestic dogs' tracks are more prevalent than ever. Although the size may vary greatly, the shape of the foot is distinctive, and that helps us to identify their tracks.

TRACKS
Front & Hind Prints: Length: 1–5" (2.5–12.7 cm)

TRACK PATTERNS
Stride: Normally erratic and focused on the movement of the dog's owner.
Comments: Several characteristics help to distinguish the domestic dog from other members of the dog family. Blunt claws and splayed toes are often present in dog tracks. The track of the domestic dog is generally less elongated, and the palm pad is larger and deeper.

SCAT
Size: Highly variable.
Comments: Dog scat is normally easy to identify as it consists largely of commercial dog food. It lacks hair, bone and other components found in the scat of the wild dog family.

HABITAT
Ubiquitous throughout the region, in rural and semi-wild locations.

SIMILAR TRACKS & SIGN
Coyote (see p. 40).
Gray Wolf (see p. 42).

Domestic dog track in sand. (BC)

Domestic Cat *Felis domesticus*

Cat Family (Felidae)
ANIMAL SIZE & WEIGHT
Total Length: 19–28" (48–71 cm)
Tail Length: 10–15" (25–38 cm)
Weight: 5–20 lb (2.3–9 kg)

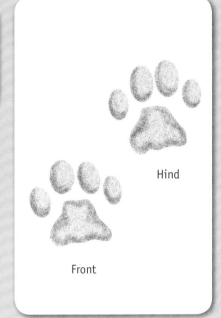

Hind

Front

The domestic cat is found in all urban areas. The tracks can be easily identified by their size and shape, as these cats seldom leave claw marks.

TRACKS
Front Print: Length: 1–1.6" (2.5–4.1 cm)
Width: 0.9–1.75" (2.2–4.4 cm)
Hind Print: Length: 1.1–1.5" (2.9–3.8 cm)
Width: 0.9–1.6" (2.2–4.1 cm)
TRACK PATTERNS
Stride: Walking: 6–12.5" (15.2–31.8 cm)
Trotting: 10–16" (25.4–40.6 cm)
Galloping: 14–40" (35.6–101.6 cm)
Straddle: Walking: 2–4.75" (5.1–12.1 cm)
Track Group Length: Galloping:
10–33" (25.4–83.8 cm)
Comments: Domestic cat tracks are much smaller than those of our native cats. The front track is larger and rounder than the rear track. As with all cats, the nails do not register while the animal is walking because they are retractable.
SCAT
Width: 1.2–2.4" (3–6 cm) in diameter
Comments: Domestic cats are well known for their habit of covering their scat.
HABITAT
Everywhere throughout the region, in urban, rural and nearby locations.
SIMILAR TRACKS & SIGN
Bobcat (see p. 66).

Domestic cat tracks in snow. (BC)

Caribou *Rangifer tarandus*

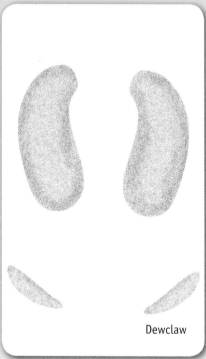

Dewclaw

Deer Family (Cervidae)
ANIMAL SIZE & WEIGHT
Total Length: 5.5–8' (1.7–2.4 m)
Tail Length: 5–9" (13–23 cm)
Weight: 200–240 lb (91–109 kg)

Caribou are found primarily in the north. In the summer months they feed on grasses, sedges, mosses, forbs, mushrooms, lichens and other foods, and in winter their diet includes buds, leaves and bark of both deciduous and evergreen shrubs, as well as arboreal lichens. Both sexes of caribou grow antlers but the male's are larger. This species' range is limited and its numbers are decreasing in several areas.

TRACKS
Front Print: Length: 3.25–5" (8.3–12.7 cm)
　　　　　　 Width: 4–6" (10.2–15.2 cm)
Hind Print: Length: 3–4.5" (7.6–11.4 cm)
　　　　　　 Width: 4–6" (10.2–15.2 cm)
TRACK PATTERNS
Stride: Walking: 23–33" (58.4–83.8 cm)
　　　　 Running: to 1.5 m (5 ft)
Straddle: Walking: 10–17" (25.4–43.2 cm)
Track Group Length: To 9' (2.7 m)
Comments: Dewclaw imprints are frequently observed with this animal's tracks. Track measurements shown here, however, do not include the dewclaws.

SCAT
Winter: Width: 0.4–0.6" (1–1.6 cm) in diameter
　　　　 Length: 0.4–0.9" (1–2.2 cm)

Deer Family (Cervidae)

Summer: 1–2.5" (2.5–6.3 cm) in diameter (patty shaped)
Comments: Both summer and winter scat resembles the scat of white-tailed deer. Winter pellets are flat or concave at one end and somewhat pointed at the other end—also similar to those of white-tailed deer.

OTHER SIGN

Beds: A simple, shallow depression is made, often in a snowbank during the summer months.
Antler Rubs: This sign is observed less frequently with caribou than with other deer species.

HABITAT

Caribou move seasonally and may inhabit lower-elevation forests much of the year, but during the summer months they move into alpine meadows and sub-alpine forest.

SIMILAR TRACKS & SIGN

Several ungulates are similar, but careful study of the track shape will show that caribou tracks are distinct.

Walking (L) & Trotting (R)

Fresh track of a caribou in sand. (AB)

73

Mule Deer *Odocoileus hemionus*

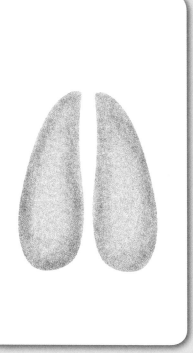

Deer Family (Cervidae)
ANIMAL SIZE & WEIGHT
Total Length: 4.5–6.2' (1.4–1.9 m)
Tail Length: 4.75–8.75" (12–22 cm)
Weight: 68–470 lb (31–210 kg)

The mule deer is named from its large, mule-like ears. This species favors mountain areas as well as open and drier country than the white-tailed deer. Historically the black-tailed deer of the Pacific Coast was classified as a distinct species, but it is now considered a subspecies of the mule deer. Its range is widespread and its numbers strong.

A bounding mule deer often speeds along with a bounding action, in which all four feet touch the ground simultaneously, with the hind feet at the rear. This distinctive gait is called a pronk.

TRACKS
Front Print: Length: 2.25–4" (5.7–10.2 cm)
Width: 1.6–2.75" (4.1–7 cm)
Hind Print: Length: 2–3.5" (5.1–8.9 cm)
Width: 1.5–2.4" (3.8–6 cm)
TRACK PATTERNS
Stride: Walking: 15–25.5" (38.1–64.8 cm)
Pronking: 8–15' (2.4–4.5 m)
Straddle: Walking: 5–10" (12.7–25.4 cm)
Track Group Length: Pronking: 30–42" (76.2–106.7 cm)
Comments: It is extremely difficult to differentiate tracks of a mule deer from those of a white-tailed deer.

Deer Family (Cervidae)

Winter scat. (WA)

Winter: Width: 0.2–0.6" (.5–1.6 cm) in diameter Length: 0.5–1.75" (1.3–4.4 cm)
Summer: 1.5–2" (3.8–5 cm) in diameter (patty shaped)
Comments: Habitat is an important clue in determining which species of deer is present in any area. Both mule deer and white-tailed deer are often present at the same site.

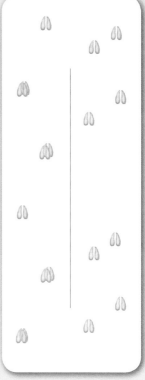

Walking (L) & Pronking (R)

OTHER SIGN

Antler Rubs: In autumn, bucks use their antlers to scar trees, shred tree bark and then rub their scent glands (on their heads and necks) onto trees to advertise their presence and readiness to breed.
Beds: Mule deer bed down for the night, often in an open area in which they feel safe.
Browse: During the winter months, deer feed on the branches of shrubs and trees. Heavy browsing can be very hard on these plants, stunting them through several years of repetitive feeding on the terminal buds.

HABITAT

In open fields, pastures, woods, groves, mixed woods to alpine tundra.

SIMILAR TRACKS & SIGN

White-tailed Deer (see p. 76).

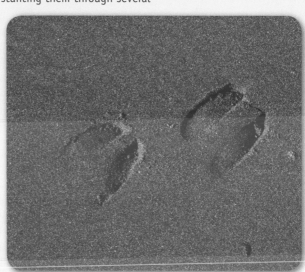

Fresh mule deer tracks in sand. (WA)

White-tailed Deer *Odocoileus virginianus*

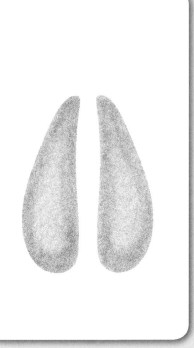

Deer Family (Cervidae)
ANIMAL SIZE & WEIGHT
Total Length: 4.5–7' (1.4–2.1 m)
Tail Length: 8.25–14" (21–36 cm)
Weight: 110–440 lb (50–200 kg)

The white-tailed deer is a common species that is widespread in its range and strong in its numbers. Its distinctive tail is raised like a flag as it bounds off into the woods. For much of the year, males stay in bachelor groups while females stay together with fawns and yearlings. Winter food is mainly the leaves and twigs of evergreen and deciduous trees and shrubs. Grasses and other forbs, including mushrooms, provide food during spring and summer. It is estimated that a white-tail will eat approximately 4.5–11 lb (2–5 kg) of food a day.

TRACKS
Front Print: Length: 1.4–4" (3.5–10.2 cm)
Width: 0.9–2.9" (2.2–7.3 cm)
Hind Print: Length: 1.25–3.5" (3.2–8.9 cm)
Width: 0.75–2.4" (1.9–6 cm)
TRACK PATTERNS
Stride: Walking: 13–26" (33–66 cm)
Bounding: 6–20' (1.5–6 m)
Trotting: 29–56" (73.7–142.2 cm)
Straddle: Trotting: 2–4" (5.1–10.2 cm)
Track Group Length:
Bounding: 10–60" (25.4–152.4 cm)
Comments: The front track is larger. In northern areas where snow is deep, deer will seek local areas where

there is less snow, to use less energy moving around. Such an area is called a deer yard.

SCAT

Winter: Width: 0.2–0.6" (.5–1.6 cm) in diameter
Length: 0.5–1.75" (1.3–4.4 cm)

Summer: 1.5–2" (3.8–5 cm) in diameter (patty shaped)

Comments: The scat measurements are so similar to those of mule deer (see p. 74) that identification based on scat measurements alone is not reliable. The hard winter pellets, consisting of wood fibres, may stay around for years.

OTHER SIGN

Browse: Since deer have incisors only on the bottom jaw, they have to tear branches rather than cut through them cleanly—unlike, for example, members of the rabbit family.

Incisor Scrapes: Incisor scrapes are made by deer scraping their lower incisors upward on a branch, resulting in no frayed bark at the bottom of the scrape.

Ground Scrapes: During the rut (the breeding season), bucks scrape the ground with their front hoofs under the overhanging branch of a nearby tree. They then bring their rear legs up near the forelegs and urinate on their own hind legs. The urine then runs down over the hock glands (located on the inside of the leg at the joint). The buck's own scent now runs down to the ground along with its urine. The deer will scent the overhanging branch with its forehead glands as well. Scent is very important for communication to females and other males in the area during the rut.

HABITAT

Valleys, streams, woodlands, meadows and similar sites with sheltered areas nearby.

SIMILAR TRACKS & SIGN

Mule Deer (see p. 74).

Walking (L) & Trotting (R)

White-tailed deer summer scat. (AB)

White-tailed deer track in sand. (NC)

Moose *Alces alces*

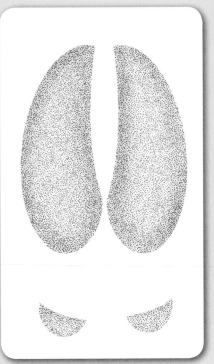

Deer Family (Cervidae)
ANIMAL SIZE & WEIGHT
Total Length: 8–10' (2.4–3 m)
Tail Length: 3.5–7.5" (8.9–19 cm)
Weight: 500–1180 lb (230–540 kg)

This large, impressive member of the deer family has been to known to reach an amazing 1800 pounds (810 kg). It is well adapted to living in snow with its long and seemingly ungainly legs.

Moose generally browse on higher shrubs—up to 7 feet (2 m) above the ground—while deer browse is usually found at 4 feet (1.2 m) and lower. The preferred browse species for moose are willow, aspen and paper birch.

TRACKS
Front Print: Length: 4.4–7" (11.1–17.8 cm)
Width: 3.75–6" (9.5–15.2 cm)
Hind Print: Length: 4.1–6.5" (10.5–16.5 cm)
Width: 3.5–4.6" (8.9–11.7 cm)
TRACK PATTERNS
Stride: Walking: 28–44" (71.1–111.8 cm)
Galloping: 4–15' (1.2–4.5 m)
Straddle: Walking: 8.5–20" (21.6–50.8 cm)
Track Group Length: Galloping: 5–10' (1.5–3 m)
Comments: Moose, like all deer, have four toes. Toes 2 and 5 are dewclaws (positioned several inches up on the back of the leg. Generally, only toes 3 and 4 register in tracks unless the substrate is very soft.

Deer Family (Cervidae)

Winter: Width: 0.5–0.9" (1.3–2.2 cm) in diameter
Length: 0.9–1.75" (2.2–4.4 cm)
Summer: 7.5–11" (19.1–28 cm) in diameter (patty shaped)
Comments: Moose scat is normally much larger than that of elk.

OTHER SIGN

Incisor Scrapes: Moose scrape aspens and other trees with their incisors. Incisor scrapes are usually at shoulder height—much higher than deer scrapes. Moose scrape in an upward motion, so individual tooth marks are visible on the bark.

Antler Rubs: Bulls rub their antlers on trees, creating smooth-looking patches similar to white-tailed deer rubs but much higher on the tree. Moose rubs may reach 90" (2.3 m) high but deer rubs are usually less than 45" (1.1 m) from the ground.

Wallows: Bulls are known to dig large wallows, in which they urinate and roll around, in autumn. Females roll in wallows as well. The wallows measure 3–10 feet (91–305 cm) long. Smaller wallows are round, and larger ones are elongated.

HABITAT

Primarily in boreal forests, often associated with wet-lands, moist woods and willow thickets.

SIMILAR SPECIES

Elk (see p. 80) have similarly shaped hooves. Size helps to determine the species in most cases.

Walking (L) & Trotting (R)

Typical winter scat of moose. (AB)

An incisor scrape on alder by a moose. (AB)

79

Elk *Cervus elaphus*

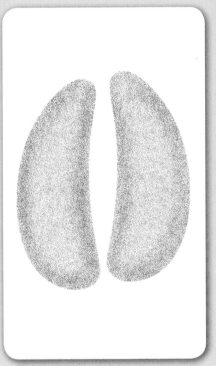

Deer Family (Cervidae)
ANIMAL SIZE & WEIGHT
Total Length: 6.5–8.5' (2–2.6 m)
Tail Length: 4.75–7" (12–18 cm)
Weight: 400–1100 lb (180–500 kg)

The elk is a large ungulate that is able to move through the forest and seemingly disappear without making a sound. This is true even for the large males with their huge racks that can measure 4' (1.2 m) across.

Males are well known for their distinctive bugling in the fall rut or breeding season. This species can be dangerous to approach. Both sexes have been known to attack anyone who ventures too close to them.

TRACKS
Front Print: Length: 3–4.9" (7.6–12.4 cm)
Width: 2.6–4.6" (6.7–11.7 cm)
Hind Print: Length: 2.5–4.5" (6.4–11.4 cm)
Width: 2.4–4" (6–10.2 cm)

TRACK PATTERNS
Stride: Walking: 18–35" (45.7–88.9 cm)
Trotting: 32–45" (81.3–114.3 cm)
Straddle: Walking: 6.75–13" (17 1–33 cm)
Trotting: 3.5–6" (8.9–15.2 cm)
Comments: Elk tracks are smaller and rounder than moose tracks; they may resemble the tracks of younger moose.

SCAT
Winter: Width: 0.4–0.7" (1–1.7 cm)
Length: 0.5–1" (1.3–2.5 cm)

Deer Family (Cervidae)

Summer scat of an elk. (AB)

Summer: 5–6" (12.7–15 cm) in diameter (patty shaped)
Comments: The winter scat of this species is one of the easiest to identify in the field.

OTHER SIGN

Antler Rubs: As with other members of the deer family, males rub their antlers against small saplings, scraping the bark off the trunks of trees. Elk rubs occur higher than white-tailed and mule deer rubs—16–72" (40–183 cm) from the ground.

Wallows: Male elk create large, muddy or dusty depressions in the ground and roll in this area after urinating in the location and on themselves. Scent is an important part of the rut.

HABITAT

Open fields, pastures, woods, groves, mixed woods and the sub-alpine meadows.

SIMILAR TRACKS & SIGN

Moose (see p. 78).

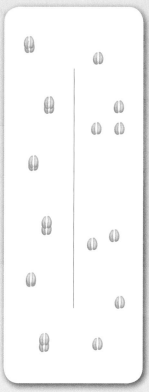

Walking (L) & Running (R)

Typical winter scat of elk. (AB)

An elk track in soft mud. (AB)

Pronghorn *Antilocapra americana*

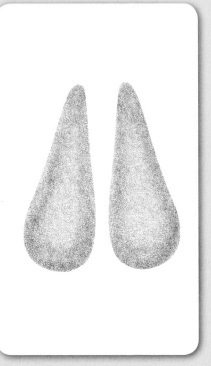

Pronghorn Family (Antilocapridae)
ANIMAL SIZE & WEIGHT
Total Length: 4–4.5' (1.2–1.4 m)
Tail Length: 3.4–6" (8.6–15 cm)
Weight: 70–140 lb (32–64 kg)

The pronghorn is unique—with pronged horns rather than antlers. They shed the outer keratin sheath each year, rather than the bony core. The pronghorn is known for several interesting behaviors. When it is annoyed or curious, it stamps with one foot and then it may deposit scat or urine on the ground. The pronghorn also produces a loud whistling sound if startled, similar to the white-tailed deer.

TRACKS
Front Print: Length: 2.1–3.5" (5.4–8.9 cm)
        Width: 1.5–2.25" (3.8–5.7 cm)
Hind Print: Length: 2.25–3.25" (5.7–8.3 cm)
        Width: 1.5–2.1" (3.8–5.4 cm)

TRACK PATTERNS
Stride: Walking (direct register): 17–26" (43.2–66 cm)
        Walking (overstep): 19–29" (48.3–73.7 cm)
        Bounding: 29–61" (73.7–154.9 cm)
Straddle: Walking (direct register): 4.4–10" (11.1–25.4 cm)
Track Group Length: Bounding: 36–82" (91.4–208.3 cm)
Comments: Pronghorn tracks are similar to those of deer, but the hind border is usually broader, and the

outside edges are normally distinctly concave. The overstep walk is also unique among ungulates.

SCAT

Width: 0.2–0.5" (.5–1.3 cm) in diameter
Length: 0.4–0.75" (1–1.9 cm)
Comments: Scats vary greatly with diet and moisture content. Summer scats are looser as a result of the high moisture content of herbaceous plants.

OTHER SIGN

Territory Marking: The pronghorn often marks its territory by scraping the ground with a hoof and then depositing scat or urine on the bare spot.

HABITAT

Open grasslands, grassy brush areas and semideserts.

SIMILAR TRACKS & SIGN

White-tailed Deer (see p. 76) and **Mule Deer** (see p. 74) tracks are very similar.

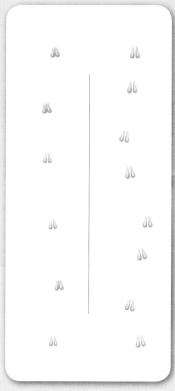

Walking (L) & Overstep Walk (R)

Track of a pronghorn. (SK)

Summer scat of a pronghorn. (SK)

American Bison *Bison bison*

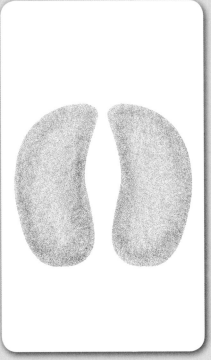

Cattle Family (Bovidae)
ANIMAL SIZE & WEIGHT
Total Length: 8–13' (2.4–4 m)
Tail Length: 11–15" (28–38 cm)
Weight: 790–2400 lb (360–1090 kg)

The well-known naturalist Ernest Thompson Seton once estimated that up to 75 million bison roamed the North American prairies before the 17th century. Today they are only found in a few parks and preserves around the continent. These large, peaceful-looking animals can be dangerous to approach during the rut or breeding season between July and October, especially around mid-August. Although they do not appear to be very fast, they can run up to 32 miles per hour (51 km/h)—faster than a wolf!

TRACKS
Front Print: Length: 4.5– 6.5" (11.4–16.5 cm)
              Width: 4.5–6" (11.4–15.2 cm)
Hind Print: Length: 4.25–6" (10.8–15.2 cm)
              Width: 4–5.5" (10.2–14 cm)
TRACK PATTERNS
Stride: Walking: 22–38" (55.9–96.5 cm)
          Trotting: 40–44" (1.02–1.12 m)
Straddle: Walking: 10–22" (25.4–55.9 cm)
           Trotting: 10–15" (25.4–38.1 cm)
Comments: The front track is rounder and larger than the rear track.
SCAT
10–16" (25.4–40.6 cm) in diameter (patty-shaped)

Cattle Family (Bovidae)

Comments: The scat closely resembles a cow patty.

OTHER SIGN

Rubs: Trees are often used as rubbing posts, and when the population of bison is high the trees are noticeably affected. Large boulders are used as well, and boulders that have been worn smooth and reshaped by thousands of bison over the centuries are still visible today, long after the bison have gone.

HABITAT

Historically, grasslands, alpine tundra and forest areas with short vegetation.

SIMILAR TRACKS & SIGN

Domestic Cattle tracks are similar except they are smaller and usually not as round.

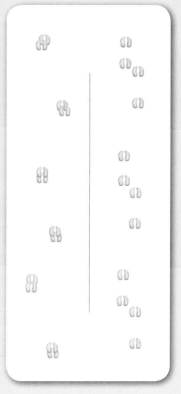

Walking (L) & Loping (R)

Bison scat resembles that of domestic cattle. (AB)

Rub trees of the American bison. (WY)

Mountain Goat *Oreamnos americanus*

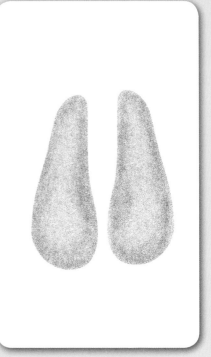

Cattle Family (Bovidae)
ANIMAL SIZE & WEIGHT
Total Length: 4–5' (1.2–1.5 m)
Tail Length: 3.5–5.5" (8.9–14 cm)
Weight: 100–300 lb (45–136 kg)

The mountain goat is a true denizen of the rugged high mountains. Shrubs are the main food, and this herbivore also feeds on grasses, sedges, rushes, mosses and lichens. Like most ungulates, it is attracted to natural salt sources and may travel long distances to reach the salt.

TRACKS
Front Print: Length: 2.5–3.5" (6.4–8.9 cm)
Width: 2.5–3.5" (6.4–8.9 cm)
Hind Print: Length: 2.5–3.25" (6.4–8.3 cm)
Width: 2.25–3" (5.7–7.6 cm)
TRACK PATTERNS
Stride: Walking: 15–30" (38.1–76.2 cm)
Straddle: Walking: 8–13" (20.3–33 cm)
Comments: The toes have a tendency to spread out, giving the track a somewhat square shape.

SCAT
Winter: Width: 0.25–0.6" (0.6–1.6 cm) in diameter
Length: 0.4–1" (1–2.5 cm)
Summer: Width: 1.5–2.6" (3.8–6.6 cm) in diameter
Length: 2–5" (5.1–12.7 cm)
Comments: The scat is very similar to that of deer and sheep, but smaller.

Cattle Family (Bovidae)

OTHER SIGN

Beds: Mountain goats scrape out shallow depressions in shale or dirt at a cliff base.

HABITAT

Steep slopes and rocky cliffs in alpine and sub-alpine areas.

SIMILAR TRACKS & SIGN

Bighorn Sheep (see p. 88).

Older tracks in dried clay. (AB)

Walking

Winter scat of a mountain goat. (AB)

Bighorn Sheep *Ovis canadensis*

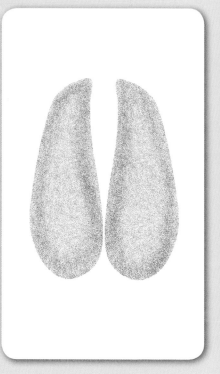

Cattle Family (Bovidae)
ANIMAL SIZE & WEIGHT
Total Length: 5–6' (1.5–1.8 m)
Tail Length: 3.25–5" (8.3–13 cm)
Weight: 120–340 lb (54–154 kg)

Seeking out a mountainous environment, this ungulate is at home in some of the most spectacular landscapes on our continent. A diet of primarily broad-leaved, non-woody plants and grasses provides the bighorn sheep with the nutrients it requires.

The rumen, or first compartment of the stomach, is larger than of a similar-sized deer, so the digestion of grasses takes longer and thus is more efficient.

TRACKS
Front Print: Length: 2.1–3.4" (5.4–8.6 cm)
        Width: 1.5–3" (3.8–7.6 cm)
Hind Print: Length: 2.1–3.25" (5.2–8.3 cm)
        Width: 1.5–2.4" (3.8–6 cm)
TRACK PATTERNS
Stride: Walking: 12–25" (30.5–63.5 cm)
        Trotting: 23–35" (58.4–88.9 cm)
Straddle: Walking: 4–11" (10.2–27.9 cm)
        Trotting: 3–6" (7.6–15.2 cm)
Track Group Length: Loping: 50–60" (1.27–1.52 m)
Comments: The hooves have straighter edges than those of deer and as a result tend to be more block-like and less pointed.

Winter scat of bighorn sheep. (AB)

SCAT
Width: 0.25–0.6" (.6–1.6 cm) in diameter
Length: 0.4–1" (1–2.5 cm)
Comments: Bighorn sheep scat ranges from dark black to gray and always has a smooth, polished finish.

OTHER SIGN
Beds: Bighorn sheep regularly bed down for the night in a slight depression that is likely to be used year after year. This site almost always smells of urine and is

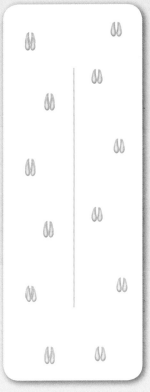

Walking (L) & Trotting (R)

edged with an accumulation of the sheep's droppings.

HABITAT
Mountainous areas where cliffs provide easy escape routes.

SIMILAR TRACKS & SIGN
Dall's Sheep *Ovis dalli* is a white sheep found from northern BC to Alaska.
Mule Deer (see p. 74).
Mountain Goat (see p. 86).

Fresh track of a bighorn sheep in soft sand. (AB)

BIRDS & OTHER WILDLIFE

Various wildlife species leave their tracks and sign as well.

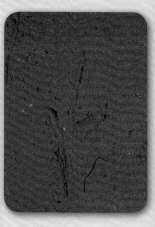

Mallard
Anas platyrhynchos
track in sand.

Killdeer *Charadrius vociferus* tracks in sand.

Great Blue Heron *Ardea herodias* track in sand.

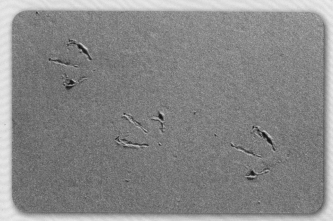

Glaucous-winged Gull *Larus glaucescens* tracks in sand.

Steller's Jay *Cyanocitta stelleri* cracked open a nut of the **beaked hazelnut** *Corylus cornuta*.

White-tailed Ptarmigan *Lagopus leucurus wing imprints in snow at takeoff.*

Boreal Toad *Bufo boreas tracks in sand.*

Beetle *tracks.*

Common Raven *Corvus corax tracks in sand.*

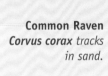

Ruffed Grouse *Bonasa umbellus tracks and wing imprints in snow.*

Glossary

amble: overstep walk.

antler rub: a location where a male ungulate rubs its antlers during the rut.

bound: a gait that involves a synchronized landing and pushing off with the hind feet.

browse: feeding on shrubs or similar woody vegetation.

cache: a store of food

den: a hole or burrow in the ground used as a home by a mammal.

dewclaws: nonfunctioning toes on mammals, located at the back of the foot too high to touch the ground.

direct register: a track pattern in which the hind foot lands directly on the track of the front foot.

gait: a manner or way of movement by an animal.

gallop: a fast mode of travel in which all four feet are off the ground at the same time.

graze: feeding on grasses or similar soft vegetation.

incisor scrape: the mark left by an ungulate when it uses its incisors to scrape bark off a tree or shrub.

lodge: the home of a mammal.

lope: a gait with a steady, regular bounding movement.

midden: a refuse heap; discarded cone scales made by squirrels and other mammals.

overstep walk: a track pattern in which the hind foot touches the ground in front of the print of the front foot but does not land directly on the print, leaving a double imprint.

predation: the killing and eating of an animal by another animal.

pronk / pronking: the distinctive bounding gait of the mule deer.

rut: the mating period for ungulates.

rut pit: a depression or pit in a damp area that is dug by an ungulate using its hooves and antlers, during the rut.

side trot: a type of overstep trot in which the hind foot is placed beside and slightly ahead of the larger front track.

sitzmark: the mark left on the ground after an animal jumps from a higher location such as a tree.

slide: a pattern of movement in which an animal moves down a slope or flat area on its belly.

straddle: the width of a full set of animal tracks.

stride: the distance from the centre of one track group to the centre of the next group.

track pattern: the distinctive repeating arrangement of tracks made when an animal moves.

trot: the gait of four-footed mammals in which the diagonal pairs of legs move forward together.

Acknowledgements & Credits

I would like to thank several people who assisted with this project.

Mary Schendlinger for her careful editing.
Jim Salt, who generously aided me in locating several species for photography.
The skilled photographers who provided photos. Their names appear below.

Dave Bates 63
Kim Cabrera 23, 59
Lyn Hart 67
Carol Roth 24
Jim Salt 54
Pamela Schreckengost 62
Susan Servos-Sept 95
Alasdair Veitch 32
Chris Wemmer 34

Bibliography

Elbroch, Mark. 2003. *Mammal Tracks & Sign: A Guide to North American Species*. Mechanicsburg PA: Stackpole Books.

Forrest, Louise Richardson. 1988. *Field Guide to Tracking Animals in Snow*. Harrisburg PA: Stackpole Books.

Forsyth, Adrian. 2006. *Mammals of North America: Temperate and Arctic Regions*. Buffalo, NY: Firefly Books.

Moskowitz, David. 2010. *Wildlife of the Pacific Northwest: Tracking and Identifying Mammals, Birds, Reptiles, Amphibians, and Invertebrates*. Portland OR: Timber Press.

Murie, Olaus J., and Mark Elbroch. 2005. *The Peterson Field Guide to Animal Tracks*, 3rd ed. New York: Houghton Mifflin.

Rezendes, Paul. 1999. *Tracking & the Art of Seeing: How to Read Animal Tracks & Sign*, 2nd ed. New York: HarperCollins.

Seton, Ernest Thompson. 1978. *Animal Tracks and Hunter Signs*. Toronto: Macmillan of Canada.

Wilson, Don E,. and Sue Ruff, eds. 1999. *The Smithsonian Book of North American Mammals*. Vancouver BC: UBC Press.

Index

About the Author

Duane Sept is a biologist, freelance writer and professional photographer. His biological work has included research on various wildlife species and service as a park naturalist. His award-winning photographs have been published internationally, in displays and in books, magazines and other publications, for clients that include BBC Wildlife, Parks Canada, Nature Canada, National Wildlife Federation and World Wildlife Fund.

Today Duane brings a wealth of information to the public as an author, in much the same way he has inspired thousands of visitors to Canada's parks. His published books include The Beachcomber's Guide to Seashore Life in the Pacific Northwest (Harbour Publishing), Wild Berries of the Northwest: Alaska, Western Canada and the Northwestern United States (Calypso Publishing) and Common Mushrooms of the Northwest: Alaska, Western Canada and the Northwestern United States (Calypso Publishing).

More Great Nature Books from
Calypso Publishing

Wild Berries of the Northwest:
Alaska, Western Canada and the Northwestern United States
J. Duane Sept

Fruits and berries are all around us. Identify these fruits and their flowers on your next trip to the ocean, lake or woods with this full-color guide. Learn which species are edible and which are poisonous. An entire chapter of mouth-watering recipes is also featured. Enjoy!

5.5" x 8.5" • 96 pages • 169 color photos
Softcover • $14.95 • ISBN 978-0-9739819-3-3

Common Mushrooms of the Northwest:
Alaska, Western Canada and the Northwestern United States
J. Duane Sept

This full-color photographic guide features 130 species of mushrooms and other fungi found in the Northwest, from Alaska to Oregon—some edible, some poisonous, all intriguing. Besides a description of each species, the book includes habitat, range, edibility, tips on distinguishing similar species and other interesting information. There are also pointers on storing edible mushrooms, making spore prints and much more.

5.5" x 8.5" • 96 pages • 150 color photos
Softcover • $14.95 • ISBN 978-0-9739819-0-2

Trees of the Northwest:
Alaska, Western Canada and the Northwestern United States
J. Duane Sept

Trees are all around us! Some live more than 1,500 years, others produce spectacular color displays in the autumn, still others have medicinal properties. More than 49 amazing species, accompanied by more than 190 full-color photos, are featured in this concise, attractive guide. Now it is easier than ever to identify—and appreciate—our fascinating trees.

5.5" x 8.5" • 96 pages • 200+ color photos
Softcover • $14.95 • ISBN 978-0-9739819-4-0

• •

These titles are available at your local bookstore or

Calypso Publishing

www.calypso-publishing.com